Selling

Above

The

Crowd

365 Strategies For Sales Excellence

By Dave Anderson

Published By Horizon Business Press
a division of Horizon Communications, Inc.

Distributed Exclusively By The Dave Anderson Corporation
P.O. Box 2338 Agoura Hills, CA 91376
Phone: 800-519-8224

Copyright May 1999 by Dave Anderson

Printed in the United States of America
Fourth Printing, 2004

ISBN # 0-9663801-3-4

DEDICATION

This book is dedicated to my mentors–past and present: Brent Haggard, Harry Patterson and John Maxwell. To my longtime friend and business associate, Mo Issa, the most capable 'right arm' anyone could ever ask for. And especially to my wife, Rhonda, and daughter, Ashley, for their support, encouragement and patience.

This book is also dedicated to the multitudes of salespeople who want to become more and contribute more to their families, their employers, their customers and themselves.

ACKNOWLEDGEMENTS

I'd like to thank my friend and fellow author, John Maxwell, for the inspiration he's provided over the years. Many thanks go to my publisher, Mike Roscoe, for his energy and direction and to my friend, Jim Boldebook, for his ideas and encouragement. Special thanks to Zig Ziglar for his unselfish insight and advice. I also want to acknowledge the throngs of salespeople and managers I've had the pleasure of working with, coaching and learning from. It was all of you who showed me what needed to be in a book on successful selling.

Preface

Selling Above The Crowd: 365 Strategies For Sales Excellence
For millions of men and women in sales today, the workplace offers little in the way of effective, on-going training or guidance to improve careers or lives. If you have the desire to pull away from the pack, raise your earnings to higher levels and derive more enjoyment out of what you do, the path to greater achievement must often be developed on your own. **Selling Above The Crowd** is your coaching guide for that journey. It offers daily steps to create the right mix of selling skills, work habits, attitude and motivation to fuel you to new levels. Whether you sell homes, insurance, automobiles, suits or computers, work in a retail outlet, network market, market a medical or accounting service, or sell from your home, **Selling Above The Crowd** provides the means to achieve results for newcomers and sales veterans alike. If you are tired of procuring average wages, falling short of your potential, and/or earning less than you need, this book is your plan to a higher plane. It is not a quick-fix! Instead, it is a career plan that you work on and improve every single day. If you're ready to start working and stop being worked, to start living instead of being lived, let's start the journey of **Selling Above The Crowd!**

The first eight chapters of **Selling Above The Crowd** lay out a foundation that the 365 Strategies build on. They are an outline of the key components that will put you on track and keep you soaring above the crowd of average sales people. Read these chapters and then begin to apply the daily strategies. Reread them several times over the next year to supplement your daily steps. The reinforcement and repetition will help develop the new mind-set, attitude, habits and skills necessary to empower you to new levels. My approach is very direct and easy to understand. No sugar-coating here. Just the straight talk and practical application you need to grow to your maximum potential. Read with a pen and highlighter handy. Highlight key points. Twice monthly, the strategies end with provisions to summarize the key points you want to apply and incorporate as part of your Action Plan. These will be the steps that take you above the crowd. **Take the time to complete the Action Plan and follow through with what you commit to!** The Action Plan will become your personal roadmap to sales excellence.

Steps Toward The Summit
Table of Contents

1

The Mandate of Attitude

Selling skills won't matter. Goals won't help. Product knowledge and knowledge of your competitor's product won't make much difference, either. Having the best product to sell won't bail you out and neither will working for the best company. The number of hours and days you put in each week won't give you an edge. Who you know won't boost your odds much, either. Hard work and good intentions will waste your time. Everything other than the right *selling attitude* is like having paper, kindling and firewood all stacked up neatly and ready to burn. Attitude is the match. You can't start the fire without it. Without the right attitude, everything else you do, plan for and hope for is consigned to mediocrity. Your growth eventually comes to a standstill. Without the right attitude, your quest for success is a roller coaster - inconsistent, undependable and frustrating. Without the right attitude, you can't build a secure future, you can't continue climbing to the next level at your job and you'll never be able to enjoy whatever fleeting success you do manage to corral for more than a flash. Sound harsh? It is...and it's true!

If attitude is the heart of our success, many salespeople need a cardiologist! For something so important to our careers, our finances and our relationships, we do a miserable job of growing, reinforcing, nurturing and protecting our attitude. Sales psychologists have said repeatedly that the right attitude accounts for 80% of success in sales. Eighty percent seems like a lot. Flip the equation around and it's the equivalent of having a paltry 20% chance of succeeding without the right attitude. How much of your time, success, happiness and future would you like riding on twenty percent odds? If life were a dress rehearsal, you might try and rationalize not going to the trouble of developing and keeping the right attitude, and if you failed, coming back and trying again. *But life is not a dress rehearsal.* You don't get to come back and recapture a moment, much less a lifetime, so let's wake up and get serious. Let's start at the beginning and grow the right attitude, guard it, and use it as a foundation to reach your dreams. Besides, you can have the best information, a great plan and super coaching, but if your head and heart are not right, you will never be able to reach your true potential because *having the right attitude is a mandate for sales success–not an option.*

In case you missed it, I'll rephrase it! You can have the best selling skills and work habits in the world, but if you are going around trying to utilize them while anchored to a lousy attitude, you're sabotaging yourself! In fact, nothing else mentioned in this book will amount to much if you don't build the right attitude and work at constantly improving it. Never forget–**attitude is a mandate, not an option!**

Growing An Attitude-A Daily Discipline

Growing an attitude is like growing most things. You have to feed it the right food. The problem is that most of us spend more time and money growing our yards than we do growing our minds. There are hundreds of books, tapes and seminars on cultivating and maintaining the right attitudes. What's discouraging is that most people in sales are so consumed with other facets of their job and lives that they ignore the area that can have maximum impact on everything else they do. Many salespeople reinforce their product knowledge or practice selling skills in sales meetings, yet leave their attitude to fend for itself. You must realign your priorities so that there's time to fortify your attitude every day. If you don't like to read, listen to tapes during your drive back and forth to work. You don't have to have a "crash course" in attitude to make an immediate difference in all you do. Begin to focus on the initial discipline and take it in doses and you'll get hooked on the benefits. The hardest thing to do is to just get started. It takes change and sacrifice. It takes walking away from your comfort zone and changing the way you view your job. It takes personal growth that raises your self-esteem. It's up to you to decide when to start and what to do. There are plenty of strategies in this book to improve your attitude but first and foremost, it's self-help.

If this seems obvious, that's great! What books have you read, tapes have you listened to, or seminars have you attended lately to beef-up your attitude? Knowing what to do is easy. **Doing it is tough!** If you've been doing it, keep it up! If not, get started…and quick! Taking the time to fortify and grow your attitude takes a refocus on daily priorities and disciplines. *You can't wait to find time to do what's most important, you have to make the time!* It's up to you to start making the time.

Grave-Diggers

If the first step to changing your thinking and attitude is fortifying your mind with motivational ideas and thoughts, the second step is being selective and protective of the other daily influences flowing into your mind on a minute-by-minute basis. Growing and maintaining the right attitude is as much what you keep out of your mind as what you put in. This book has a series of daily disciplines to keep you focused on your success. All of these steps work, especially when cumulated together and used on a consistent, daily basis. They will take root faster and create more value if you keep the "grave-diggers" away. Grave-diggers are forces we encounter every day that slow our progress and have the potential to wipe it out completely. We call them grave-diggers because they have the ability to bury your career, your future and, ultimately, bury you alive. Soon after anyone begins to get ahead and rise above the crowd, grave-diggers zero in and begin to tear down if preventive measures are not taken. First, let's identify characteristics of grave-diggers and their actions.

At every workplace in the world there are negative people possessed by negative attitudes, living mostly uninspired and miserable existences. They go to work to "wait" for something to happen in their careers and in their lives. For the most part they have no goals, little ambition and spend most of their time justifying being average by blaming everyone and everything else. Based on the way they criticize and find fault, you'd think they were being paid for it. To all outward appearances, they seem to be pretty nice folks; on the inside, though, they're miserable. Misery loves company and if anyone starts to excel or pass them by, grave-diggers turn into piranhas, chewing them up and trying to bring them down to their level. This group would rather discuss than decide anything. They'd rather *study* the race than *join* the race. They're filled to the brim with excuses to explain away their lack of achievement. They think that anyone more successful than they are has had all the breaks and are content to wait indefinitely for theirs to come. Most of this group shows up at the job every day without a vision, a plan or a peep of what might happen that day. They hold their breath, relying on the cards they are dealt, hoping that one day four aces might just show up. For the most part, they know they're going nowhere fast in life but are more comfortable with old problems than they are with new solutions. New solutions would mean change, and grave-diggers are so blinded by the cost of doing something–change–that they lose sight of the cost of doing nothing. The cost of doing nothing is staggering, both for the grave-digger and for the company employing them. We sometimes make the mistake of believing that if we don't actively associate with grave-diggers at work and just listen to, but don't partake in their cancerous conversations or actions, that we're safe from their effects. After all, we don't want to offend anyone. And what harm is there if we just nod sympathetically while they rattle off their negativism, passively listening to their gossip and self-justification? Surely that's not hurting anything. WRONG! Just being around grave-diggers is subliminal poison for the attitude. It's like second-hand smoke. Just being in the same room with it can make you sick. It gets on you, in your clothes and into your hair and lungs. Even after you leave the smoky area, you still have it on you and in you. You smell like someone else's problem-even though you weren't the one smoking.

It is a proven fact that second-hand smoke will eventually kill you. Grave-diggers eventually kill your career and your future. Look for a support group at your job; one that has the same values and attitudes as yourself. Avoid everyone and everything else. Wise supervisors realize that the biggest threats to their organization come from the inside and not the outside. Supervisors who don't try to fix and then terminate grave-diggers and their activities are part of the problem and their days are numbered in any progressive organization. If any of these characteristics sound familiar to the extent they are describing *your activities*–if you have been a grave-digger in the workplace, realize that you need an immediate change of self to clear the way for the positive change and results you are seeking.

Grave-diggers are certainly not limited to the workplace. They can be found lurking in social clubs, church, circles of friends and family. Their closeness to you does not reduce their poison; it intensifies it. Your guard has to be up around the clock. It may take a while, but if you'll avoid being drawn into conversations and activities where grave-digging permeates, those around you will get the message. Stay above it. Stay focused and keep your armor of attitude on alert for these assaults. Recognize them and avoid them. Confront them when necessary. Remove yourself from unacceptable situations and conversations. Stay on the high road–above the crowd. The low road leads straight to the graveyard.

Nowhere To Hide

Factor in all the positive and negative influences. Factor in good and bad days, highs and lows, and ups and downs. The bottom line is that you are responsible for choosing your attitude. Regardless of what happens to you, it's *how* you handle it that counts. As tempting as it might be to blame a bad attitude on circumstances, that's the easy way out and it won't fly. You have the freedom to choose your attitude in any situation and in the face of any circumstance. No passing the buck. No passing the blame. The buck and the blame stop with you; how you take it and how you respond–with what you do and say. Once you grow up emotionally and accept responsibility for this, you can deal effectively with maintaining and developing your attitude, taking your success or lack of it into your own hands, and realizing that it's up to you; there's *nowhere to hide.* Too many things that happen at work are classified as "problems" and reacted to accordingly. "Problems" like losing a deal, having an upset customer, getting chewed out by the boss, etc., are not real problems at all. They are just conditions of being in the sales profession. These things are going to happen and it's not the things that are the problem. It's what you let them do to you. Do you let one lost sale affect your attitude so forcefully that you blow your next two or three opportunities? How many times has a negative encounter with a supervisor ruined your day to the point where you accomplished nothing the rest of the day? ***Don't allow five-minute conversations to ruin an eight-hour day!*** The manner in which you react–how you take it–is the problem. The events themselves are just a condition. Get used to them and learn to deal with them. They are part of the business. When it comes to having the right attitude and keeping the most productive influences at the center of what you do, you have two choices: performance or excuses. You get to choose which you'll accept for yourself. Performance is tougher, but it pays much better. Only after you accept responsibility for this choice can you move onto the next step in rising above the crowd.

2

Goals That Go!

Your parents probably didn't teach you how to set goals. You don't learn about goals in school, either. Yet by the time you get to the workplace, you are asked what yours are, even though chances are that no one at any job you ever had showed you how to set them. Since goals are so poorly explained and regarded in such generic terms, we need some defining criteria to determine exactly what they are, what they do, and how to set them. By default, goals not properly set, planned for and committed to, end up as merely good intentions. Are you a goal-setter? If you answered "yes," are you sure? Here is what separates wishful thinking from goal setting. Goals are *written* down. Goals have a step-by-step, *written* plan on how they will be reached. Goals have precise *written* deadlines. Goals are specific. Goals have factored in potential obstacles and are set with a commitment and no option for failure. Goals are realistic and achievable. Based on this criteria, are you a legitimate goal-setter or a "king of wishful thinking?" If you are a "king of wishful thinking," you're not alone. It's estimated that only three percent of the population sets goals the right way. Most people only have goals in their head, and those don't count as anything but good intentions.

What Goals Do

Now that we know more about what real goals are, let's talk about what they can do for you. David Jensen, while Chief Administrative Officer for The Crump Institute of Biological Imaging for the UCLA School of Medicine, did a study of attendees at Zig Ziglar's Success Seminars around the country. He divided them into two groups: those who set goals and developed a plan of action to reach them, and those who took no action to set goals. The studies showed that the goal-setters earned an average of $7,401 each month, compared to the non goal-setters who earned $3,397. Said Jensen, "These results also confirm the academic literature on goals that, over the past 20 years, has shown unequivocally that those who set goals perform better in a variety of tasks."

When you consider that proper goal setting forces you to think about what you want to do, empowers you to put a detailed plan together on how you'll get there rather than leaving it to chance, and holds you accountable to a specific deadline for getting where you want to go, it's no wonder that the goal-setters made more than twice the money that the non goal-setters did.

Unfortunately, most people show up every day at work with no real clue of what they expect to accomplish and certainly no plan on how they'll do it. They wake up, hold their breath, cross their fingers and hope something good will happen or hope nothing bad happens. They have good intentions but end up leaving their destiny to chance. The fact is that we live in times that have too little focus and concentration. The poet Goethe said that the key to success in life is concentration and elimination. Concentrating on the things we want and eliminating distracting, non-productive activities along the way. Most salespeople do neither. For the most part, we all want to try a little bit of everything. We live our lives like a shotgun shell, hoping that if we scatter in enough directions we might hit the target. A study by USA Today showed that the average 55 year old male in the U.S. had $2,300 in his lifetime savings. He worked long and probably worked hard for over 30 years. It's also safe to say he had good intentions and expected to have more. What he missed was planning, focus and a commitment to fulfill a plan. Most people spend more time planning Christmas or a vacation than they spend planning their careers and their lives. What a shame that sports teams have a detailed plan on how they will play a game and the average person doesn't have a plan for what he wants out of life!

Getting Started

Proper goal setting can keep us focused and help us design a career and a better life. The question is, how do we do it? Most workplaces expect you to set goals and have forecasts for your performance, even though they probably never showed you how to set them or reach them. We end up "ball parking" and failing and resigning ourselves to the belief that goal setting is a mesh of "feel good" hype that doesn't work. We've talked about what real goals are and have touched on what they can do for us. Let's talk about how to set them. Goals should be set in all areas of your life, but as this is a book on bettering your selling career, we'll focus on professional goals.

1. Determine Where You Are: At sales seminars across the country, when I ask groups of salespeople to raise their hands if they want their closing ratios to increase, everyone quickly raises their hand. Then I ask if they want their percentage of repeat and referral business to increase and everyone's hand goes up again. When I ask the group to keep their hand up if they know what their current closing ratio and percentage of repeat and referral business is, **everyone's hand goes down!**

Step one in setting effective goals or planning any improvement is to know where you are now. If you don't know where you are, how can you reach a new destination? How can you measure progress? How do you know, for sure, if you are getting better or worse? A car salesman who averages ten car sales per month by talking to 50 customers has a 20 percent closing ratio(10/50=20%). Over the next 90 days his sales jump up to an average of 12 per month. He got better, right? Maybe, maybe not. What if he had to wait on 80 customers to sell the 12---his closing ratio actually dropped to fifteen percent didn't it (12/80=15%)? On paper he looked like he had improved. He certainly felt like he had improved and had probably even made more money. The reality is, if he didn't track and know where he was starting from, he is blind to the fact that he is regressing and probably headed for trouble in his career. Tracking is paramount to knowing where you really are. The maxim is simple: anything you want to improve, you should track. Studies have shown that simply *measuring* an individual's performance *improves* performance, regardless of what is done with the measurements. If you don't want to improve an area, simply don't bother tracking and you won't improve, at least not on any consistent basis. Most salespeople don't track at all; many don't track enough. They leave their "progress" to gut feelings of how they think they're doing. The most important thing to remember about tracking is that you have to do it before you can set realistic and achievable goals. In fact, tracking is a prerequisite to goal setting.

The second important thing to remember is how far back to go in order to get a clear picture of where you really are. The most effective tracking time frame is your most recent 90-day performance. Anything prior to that is ancient history. It may be helpful to look further back to identify trends, but not for determining where you *really* are and for setting realistic goals. For example, let's take our car salesperson friend again. The past six months his sales were: 20, 20, 20, 10, 10, 10, for a total of 90 sales in a six month period. This would give him a six month average of 15 cars per month. If he were getting ready to set a goal for the next month, based on his 15 car average he would probably set his goal at 17 or 18. He would also probably fail to meet his goal. This is because his most recent history, the past 90 days, reflects a total of 30 sales for an average of 10 units per month. A 70-80% increase in one month would not be a realistic or achievable goal for most salespeople. Setting goals too high is almost as bad as setting them too low.

This is how we get set up to fail every day in our careers. We look back too far and lose focus of our most recent performance. Then we set an unrealistic goal and fall short. The preamble to effective goal setting is waking up to the fact that we need to know where we really are in our most recent career performance. We tend to color our thoughts with glory days of the past and remember our best month, or look too far back and find the rut we were in and set our goals based on information that is either too high or too low.

Suggested areas to track in sales, depending on what you are selling are: closing ratio overall per product (for simplistic purposes, your closing ratio is the number of sales you make divided by the number of prospects you talk to). You can also track the percentage of business you derive from repeat and referral customers, your ratio for phone calls made or taken versus appointments set, the ratio of appointments set versus those who actually show up, the closing ratio for those who show up from appointments (see how it differs from "walk-in" traffic), your average commission on each type of product you sell, average amount of each sale, your closing ratio after a customer leaves without buying and you get them in again and sell them (be-backs), closing ratio on customers who are referred to you from other people, closing ratio on repeat customers, ratio of sales you are able to sell from stock rather than order or trade for, and the list goes on and on. Remember the maxim: *Don't bother tracking anything unless you want to improve it.* And if you doubt the importance of knowing where you are before trying to get where you want to go, the next time you're ready to take an airplane trip, call your travel agent and tell him your desired destination, how you want to get there, when you want to leave for the trip and when you want to arrive. When the agent asks you where you are starting from, tell him you don't know. See if he can get you where you want to go.

2. Putting Your Goals To Work: Steps To Effective Goal Setting

Brainstorm about what you want to have and what you want to accomplish. Get away from phone calls, televisions, other people and every other distraction for awhile and spend some quiet time just thinking deeply about what you want. We get into such a hurry these days that we spend more time reacting than really thinking about what it is we are after, what will have the most meaning for us, where we want to wind up in life. After you have determined where you are, it's important that you start to put together a clear picture of where you want to be.

In simplest terms, the goal setting process is as follows:
• Determine where you are.
• Visualize where you want to go.
• Put a plan together to get you from where you are to where you want to go.
• After you write down the goals you want to achieve, write the date of when you want to get there.

Next, to determine if your goals are realistic or not, put a time line together with progress points figured for where you have to be each step of the way. For instance, if your goal is to save $5,000 in a year's time, break it down and determine where you need to be each month in order to stay on track. If it's not feasible to save $416.67 per month, then adjust your goal to a reasonable amount. This may sound basic, but it's often overlooked. We often set goals based on "gut" feelings rooted in overconfidence. In this case, we need to examine the dollars and cents reality and decide if we can manage the $416.67 per month as probable or a pipe dream. Is it realistic to have $2,500 of the $5,000 saved after six months, $1,250 after three months, etc. *Here's a flash;* if you don't feel deep inside that you can reach the goal and are going strictly with emotion, you'll miss. You can fool yourself but you can't fool the numbers. If you can't see it realistically, there's no way you'll ever achieve it. When you set dates for reaching your goals, always set the longest term goals first and then break them down into a series of short term goals to be attained along the way. This series of short term goals will get you to your long term goals when you follow the next few steps.

Now that you have the goals and the deadline, it's time to do the most important part; put together the plan to get you to the goal. *In actuality, goals are a dime a dozen. The plan is where the money's at.* It's easy to say, "I want to have $100,000 in the bank in two years. Figuring out how to get there and then following through and doing it is where most goal-setters with good intentions fall down. We are a society that plans sparingly. Most of us really do spend more time planning the Holidays or a weekend getaway than we spend planning our career or our retirement. The fact is, most successful people in life and business have definite plans to go with their goals. How many successful people do you know who became successful because they "just made it up as they went along?" Ridiculous, isn't it? Planning is the tough part because it involves real thinking and calculating. It goes beyond just writing things on a wish list. It forces you to commit specifically about how you'll make it happen. It puts you out on a limb and outside your comfort zone. A plan means you have to take action and do something and stop hoping something good will happen to you. Another function of a plan is that, as you put one together, you can begin to visualize the path needed to reach your goal–it makes it real. A plan keeps you on track over time and through obstacles. It should be a measuring stick for progress and a guidepost for your commitment. It will prompt you into action and keep you moving in the right direction. **Any plan that doesn't force you to take action toward your goal isn't worth the paper it's written on.** Take the time to put a solid plan together for each goal you have; a plan which is realistic, believable and one that you can see yourself working.

Too often, when we fall short of our goal, it's not necessarily the goal that is the problem–it's the plan we put together to get there. When you set a realistic goal and see yourself falling short of reaching it, don't automatically second-guess the goal itself. Go back and evaluate the plan. Is it viable? Effective? Are you working it the right way? If not, leave the goal alone and go back to rework the plan for reaching it. It's been estimated that setting the goals accounts for twenty-five percent of the effectiveness in reaching them. The other seventy-five percent is made up of developing the plan, following it with persistence and adjusting it when necessary. It's where the real work comes in.

It's now time to commit to success with no excuses, and to make the journey fun. By now you should have realistic, achievable, written goals. Add to that a deadline for completion, a series of short-term goals to lead you to your long-term goals and a calculated, specific plan to get you there. To complete the process, let's talk about eliminating excuses for failure. You should factor in obstacles and possible glitches in the process *before* you set the goal, so that if and when they do come up, you won't seize the opportunity to bail out of the goal and justify not hitting it. When you set a realistic and achievable goal and have a sound plan to get there you have to stick with it and persevere as circumstances arise. Yes, it may become necessary to make a course change or rework the plan or goal down the road, but you shouldn't make it your first option when things get tough. Factor in any potential roadblocks so that when you write down the goal, you do it with conviction and with full intention and belief of hitting it, regardless of bumps in the road. Sticking with a goal is not an issue of talent or intelligence. It's an issue of heart and persistence. Amway co-founder Rich deVos describes persistence as "stubbornness with a purpose." That's the mentality you must adopt when pursuing your goals and the tenacity you must maintain when working through the inevitable bumps along the way to achieving them. As for making goal setting fun, try to refrain from the tendency to turn goal setting into a "death march," where you set your goal, hold your breath, put your head down and begin plodding toward the mark. What a grind! Instead, as you reach short-term goals on the way to the main goal, you should reward yourself. Whether the rewards are large or small is irrelevant. They should be spelled out ahead of time and fulfilled when you reach the point of achievement. The journey to a goal should be just as enjoyable and meaningful as the destination. *The road to reaching your goals should be motivating, not intimidating.*

Remember to stay focused along the way. One of the biggest pitfalls of goal setting is *forgetting* about the goals. It sounds ridiculous, but it happens to most goal-setters at one time or another. You write your goals down, put them in a book, set it aside and go back to working toward them out of your head. You lose sight of your goals and plans when you do this. Your goals need to be reviewed, and often. As human beings, we move toward what we think about. Our mind completes pictures it can see. When goals are out of sight, they are literally out of mind. You lose the momentum and focus needed to succeed.

How often should you review your goals and plans? It depends on how badly you want to reach them. The more you review and focus, the faster you get there. Today's pace of living makes it easy to get sidetracked. If you are serious about goal setting, you have to accept that there is a lot of daily competition for your attention–and if goals are not within sight, they are easily put on the back shelf and soon turn into daydreams. Daily diligence in reviewing and working on our goals has to become a priority. **Don't wait until you find the time to do what's most significant. Make the time!**

Now for a word about the absolute toughest part of goal setting; *getting started*. Too often we hear ideas on subjects like goal setting and nod our heads in agreement, realize it makes sense and then wait for the perfect time to change what we are doing and implement it. **There is no perfect time to change or start. So go ahead and do it now!** Some of us are stuck so deeply in the warmth of our routine that our comfort zone has turned into a dead zone. Instead of going out on a limb and looking for fruit, we've chained ourselves to the tree trunk and never veer from where we are at ease. Part of the problem is that we feel no urgency to set goals. There is no immediate "pain" if we don't do it. It's like the difference between throwing a frog in a pot of boiling water or putting it in a pot of water at room temperature and slowly turning up the heat. If you throw the frog in boiling water it will jump out quickly! There is pain and urgency to change its environment. On the other hand, when you place it in the pot of room temperature water and turn up the heat gradually, the frog adjusts slowly to the heat, gets comfortable, falls asleep and pretty soon is cooked. The frog never sees it coming. People are the same way. There is no physical pain if they don't set goals, so they stay in their room-temperature routine. As the heat gets turned up throughout a life of reacting, poor planning and going through the motions, they adjust, get comfortable again and continue to cope rather than change. Pretty soon they are cooked; burned out, at a dead end, so deep in a rut they can't find a way out. Suddenly, they feel panic to change their careers, their marriage, and their lives overall when chances are more likely they need a change of *self* a lot more than they need a change of scene. Waiting for the perfect time to begin your goal setting wastes the one thing you cannot afford to throw away–time. Your lifeline of time is just like a taxicab meter. It keeps running whether you are standing still or moving forward.

When it comes right down to it, goal setting is going to cost you something, one way or another. It's going to take time, focus and money for books, seminars, and tapes. You may have to give up something else in order to have time to do it properly; *you may have to give up to go up.* The problem is that you can get so caught up over the cost of doing something that you lose sight of the cost of doing nothing. The cost of doing nothing in today's market is staggering! There's too much money, opportunity and potential being left on the table to justify waiting any longer to get serious about goal setting. It's a first step and the foundation to all success you can attain in life. Proper goal setting affords you the opportunity to design your career and your life rather than allow your career and life to design you. One last word on goal setting - start from the inside out. It is natural to set "outside" goals. Goals that are focused on tangibles; money, possessions, vacations, position, etc. However, if you want to have greater success reaching these outside goals, set "inside" goals to help you get there. Inside goals are goals for more discipline, patience, compassion, persistence and the like. You often have to develop these traits through seminars, books or tapes that address these areas. Inside goals are easily overlooked while we pursue the tangibles. The fact is, it's going to be tougher to hit the higher level tangibles if we stay at the same level inside. Sir Edmond Hillary said that after he became the first person to climb Mount Everest, "I had to conquer *myself* before I could conquer the mountain."

Inner development has to come before you can maximize *outer* achievement. Too many of us wait around for our job to get better or for conditions to improve. Your job will get better only as *you* get better and you get better when you go to work on yourself, from the inside out.

3

Daily Maximum Impact

There is no question that setting solid goals and following effective plans will help keep you focused, motivated, and in the achievement mindset. However, you will achieve your goals more quickly and more enthusiastically if you can do so by working smarter, not just by working harder or longer. Most of us in the sales profession work plenty of long, hard hours. The key to moving above the crowd in your selling career is in making better use of the time you have. You should have a goal to get more done in less time so that you leave work, go home, have a well-rounded life and avoid the burnout and grind that is associated with overachieving in sales. Calculate the total hours you spend at work in a given day. Now determine the actual hours you spend doing something directly related to creating a sale. If you're like most salespeople across the country, you spend only one third of your time actually creating sales. Your goal should be to plan each day in advance and fill it with selling activities so that you are always doing something that will either create a sale today or somewhere down the road. There is a sign that hangs over the Phoenix Suns' locker room: "The game is scheduled, we have to play it–we might as well win." ~ *Bill Russell, Boston Celtics*. If you have to be at work anyway, plan it for maximum sales creation and play it to win.

Part of the problem with a lack of planning is that too many of us come into work with a "lottery mindset." We hope that today is the day that our number comes up. The majority of salespeople come to work to wait for something to happen. They hold their breath, cross their fingers and rely on good intentions to produce the results they need for success. They have no real plan for the day and spend much of their time going through the motions. Then they wonder why today is so much like yesterday, and the day before, and the month before and so on. When we have no focus or plan for the day, the slightest distraction or crisis can get us off track. When you don't have a plan to shape your day, you end up being shaped by what happens during the day.

In our "busyness," we confuse activity with accomplishment and are exhausted at day's end, having achieved little or nothing. Another average day in an average career. Sound a little familiar?

Let's begin addressing the problem by going over three steps to get the maximum impact out of each day you have. **These three steps are a key to achieving Daily Maximum Impact:**

(1) Complete your day before it begins
(2) Budget time to improve
(3) Evaluate and adjust

(1) Complete Your Day Before It Begins

Having no plan for a day can be a disaster. Some of us take a step in the right direction by planning it in the morning or when we get to work. However, to derive maximum impact we have to go a step further than that. We need to plan it the night before. The problem with waiting until you come to work to start filling your planner or "to do" list is that many times the minute you hit the door at the office, activities take hold of you and don't let go until late in the morning or afternoon, i.e., meetings, important phone calls to return, customers who call with problems, etc. Waiting until you get to work to set your course for the day is too late; the ship has already pulled up anchor and is headed out to sea with the map and compass back on the dock. As you wrap up Monday, you should have Tuesday well thought out and planned before you ever leave the office. This is simplified by using a planner. Then, when you walk into work on Tuesday, you already have a focus and direction for the day. Your blueprint is in hand and you can hit the ground running. There's nothing quite like getting off to a good start in the morning. It sets the tone for the entire day. (The best thing about a good start is that you never have to recover from it.) Sure, you may need to make course corrections throughout the day as events arise, but corrections are more easily made with a plan already in place that you can work around. Start completing your day before it begins and see your confidence soar as you approach the new day. You'll also enjoy a job more when you feel you have more control and a tighter grip on what is happening. It sure beats coming in and reacting to what the day has to throw at you without ever getting a chance to gain any momentum toward what you want to do. Isn't if funny that the one activity which has the most profound effect on your success, sales creation, is always subordinated to the daily "emergencies" which are always popping up? Don't let it happen. Plan your day the day before.

It's been estimated that one hour of planning saves three hours of execution. In reality, you should only need 10-15 minutes to map out each day. Based on a five-day work week, that will add up to enough time in planning to buy you back that three hours of execution. That's twelve hours per month. That's like having another day and a half each month to be productive and make more sales. What a great way to gain an edge without having to work any harder or longer–just a little smarter. Once you get good at completing your day before it begins, you can do the same for a week, month and year.

(2) Budget Time To Improve

The second step to getting the maximum impact out of each day is to budget time to improve yourself every day. Sometimes we think that just by showing up at our job we are automatically getting better at what we do. We think that the more time we put in and the more experience we get, the smarter and better we become. If you rely totally on time and experience to make you better, you're in real trouble! Time and experience will help you improve, but soon you plateau and level off if you're not making a conscious effort to improve and develop your skills on a daily basis. Think of some of the people you know in sales who have been at it along time. Are there newer people in the business who outsell them? Probably. Are the "old timers" selling several times more than they were a few years ago or are they producing pretty close to the same numbers? Chances are they stopped developing or acquiring new skills after only a few months in the business, after the initial training and orientation ran out. It's common for salespeople to try to use the skills they learned the first few months in the business and run an entire career with them. This is why there are so many average salespeople in the selling profession. As a professional salesperson you have to realize that the business is not just going to come along and improve you. You can't just wait for the business to get better. Remember, it gets better when you get better and you only get better when you go to work on yourself and your skills.

There are three areas all salespeople should work on and improve every day: **Selling Skills, Product Knowledge and Attitude & Motivation.**

Selling Skills. What are some of the new closes you've learned in the past 30 days? 60 days? Year? Five Years? How about techniques for overcoming objections, prospecting and follow-up, negotiation methods, etc.? There are literally dozens of selling skills for sales professionals to learn and develop. It takes repetition, practice, drilling and rehearsing to make them reflexive. You can't just listen to a training tape, watch a video or read a book to learn these techniques to the extent that they become internalized in your sales arsenal. There are no shortcuts to developing selling skills. Decide on which area you want to work on first. Take one skill or one technique at a time and work on it a **minimum** of 30 minutes per day. Once you have mastered it, move on to another skill. Don't use the "shotgun" approach and try to take a crash course and learn too much at once. You won't retain enough of the material. **When developing new skills, don't fear going slowly; fear standing still.** Role play with another salesperson to get the kinks worked out. It won't cost you a dime if you make a mistake while practicing the script with a peer, but it could cost you a sale if you botch a newly learned close in front of a customer. Too many salespeople "wing it" when they're with a customer. They aren't prepared and they miss sales because of it. Everyone wants to be more successful in sales but few are willing to prepare for it. *The level of your practice will determine the level of your performance.* Take it slow and develop your skills on a consistent, perfected basis. Think in long range terms and be patient with your progress. Remember when practicing, repetition overcomes adversity and preparation reduces stress when you are with a customer. More preparation and less stress equals more skills and increased confidence which, in turn, produces the additional sales needed to propel you to the next income level in your career.

Product Knowledge. Do you know enough about your product/service or are you bluffing your way through presentations with too many customers? It's vital to know enough about your product/service to present the features, advantages and benefits and get your customers excited about owning it. As part of your study, you should also be learning about your competition–not so you can knock it, but so that you can point out the advantages yours has in specific areas over your major competitors and avoid the areas where it may fall short. The key to powerful product presentation is not to simply point out the features-anyone can do that. You gain the professional edge when you can also explain the advantage of the feature (what it does) and the benefit to your customers (what it means to them). Just pointing out the features raises the cost of owning the product. Explaining the advantages and benefits raises the value in owning it. As a consumer, when are you prepared to pay more–when you see more cost or value? You feel better when you see more value and so do your customers. Take a look at the difference in presenting the product in the following scenario by **Boring Bob** who just presents features, and a professional sales presentation by **Value Vinny** who explains advantages and benefits:

Boring Bob: *"Mr. Jones, the new Ford Taurus you're looking at has an anti-lock braking system, remote control entry and a stainless steel exhaust."*

Value Vinny: *"Mr. Jones, the new Taurus has anti-lock brakes. They'll give you more controlled stopping in slick or icy surfaces so you* *can maintain control of your car and make it safer for your wife and daughter, and I know safety is one of your primary concerns, isn't it? It also comes with a remote entry feature. Just hit this button and the doors are unlocked and waiting for you by the time you get up to them, which will really come in handy on those rainy days or when your hands are filled with packages, won't it? Think of how much safer Mrs. Jones is going to be getting into her car in parking lots at night not having to fumble around for her keys. It's hard to put a price on that kind of peace of mind isn't it, Mr. Jones? Let me point out this stainless steel exhaust system. Because of it's construction, it lasts much longer and won't wear out over time which increases its dependability and decreases the cost to maintain the car, both of which you are concerned with, aren't you?"*

No comparison is there? Therefore, when studying your product, don't stop at focusing on the features. You'll also want to be able to communicate the *advantage* and *benefit* of each feature to the customer. This will take diligent study and practice. This would be a great place to start with your 30 minutes per day of product study. It's estimated that eighty percent of buying and selling takes place in the presentation of a product. In that case, it would really make sense to put some more power and value into your presentations, wouldn't it? Start by learning features of the product that you sell and features of the competition's product. Then practice converting the advantages and benefits of the features. Work through your entire product line and stay current on changes in your product. One more important note on product knowledge: *While you need to know everything about what you are selling, it's not necessary to dump all of that information on each customer you have.* Every customer has buying motives or "hot buttons." Find out from your customer what they are and focus on them. Otherwise, you wind up overloading the customer with too much information and can talk them out of a sale (by making them question whether they really need everything you're talking about). Overloading can also cause your customer to go home and "think it over," because with all the information you've imparted, you've turned it into a bigger decision than they thought. **Remember, it's great to know your product, but you can't bore people into buying.** Find out what makes them "tick" and sell towards those motives. You'll create more urgency, more excitement and more sales. When you combine superior product knowledge with selling skills you'll be developing at the same time; get ready to watch your income soar!

Attitude & Motivation. Most of us in sales realize that there are numerous selling and product skills that need to be learned and developed over a long period of time. That doesn't necessarily mean we work on them as we should, but we are aware of the improvement needed in these areas and will attend workshops and take courses to hone our abilities. Sometimes, however, we seem to get the idea that our attitude and motivation will just take care of themselves. If attitude is eighty percent of what we do in sales, it makes sense to work on it just as hard, if not more so, than the other areas we focus on. There are a number of tapes and books that can be read and applied to our life and job. Bookstores are filled with more mind food than one could ever absorb. What we need are daily doses of attitude and motivation reinforcement. The pace and emotion of an average day swings too widely not to pay constant attention to keeping yourself mentally on track. Working on goals and preparing and reviewing plans to reach the goals are also exercises that you can invest your 30 minutes per day doing. You have to prepare your mind to drive through the obstacles and hurdles that present themselves as well as establish the state of mind that allows you to function and prosper in positive and negative circumstances alike. Every time you are beaten down by a negative thought or setback due to limited inner belief and esteem, you are killing your paycheck on the installment plan. As John Wooden said, "Things turn out best for those who make the best of how things turn out." You have to be mentally prepared to turn unfavorable circumstances into opportunities every hour of every day. Working on your attitude and motivation *daily* will condition you to remain sharp and focused so you can respond reflexively and convert whatever happens into an opportunity. Working on your attitude and motivation also eliminates the *mental flabbiness* that leads to mediocrity.

(3) Evaluate And Adjust

Sometimes we rush from one day to the next, to the next week and to the next month in a total blur. Each day offers a wealth of feedback on how to make the next one better. Yet we rarely take the time to look at the feedback and apply the lessons learned to making the next day more productive. Just as any sports team reviews their game films to look for problems to correct and positives to reinforce, you should review the snapshot of your day and factor in course corrections and changes to make tomorrow a better day. You should then include those adjustments when planning for your next "game." While you live your career-path looking ahead, you can learn from it by looking back, briefly, without dwelling.

4

Why Focusing On Closing Is Overrated, Overdone & Killing Your Paycheck

Every salesperson, manager and owner of a business likes to talk about closing the sale. We all know strong "closers." There are a number of books and tapes on how to close more sales and there are some people in all organizations who are regarded as weak at closing. We could fill the pages of this book with dozens of different closing words and phrases, but there are a number of books available filled with closing verbiage. (I've enclosed a list of recommended reading material on page 197 of the book.) The important question is how effective those closing words or phrases will be at bailing you out of the following: a bad first impression, failure to build a rapport with the customer, not taking the time to investigate wants and needs properly, not determining "hot buttons" and subsequently presenting a product that may be wrong for the customer, an overall failure of the customer to like, listen, trust and respect you. Closing, as we think of it, is *important* but for professionals in sales, closing is not "Step 10" on the road to the sale. Closing is not getting to a certain point, shutting your eyes, making a wish and blurting out a "closing question." Closing is anything you do that has a positive effect on the sale from the moment the customer sees you. You are closing through the entire process. Too many salespeople fail to do the first part of the sale right (make a good first impression, meet and greet, build rapport, investigate, present the product, demonstrate the product, etc.) and hope that the "tricky" closing techniques they learned will make the sale for them. It doesn't work that way. The only way that comes close to working is if you can make the product cheap enough so that customers go ahead and buy it in spite of you. With commission sales, this makes for a short, miserable and unprofitable career!

Improving Your Closing

So how do you get better at closing? Start by getting better at meeting and greeting the customer. Make an impacting first impression. Take the time to build rapport with your customer. *Slow down and invest time, diagnosing their needs before prescribing solutions.* Think of other professionals you know, e.g., doctors, attorneys, CPA's, etc. What type of fact finding do they do before they suggest a remedy? A doctor doesn't just look you over and write a prescription. An attorney doesn't greet you, make a little small talk and then recommend that you plead guilty. Professionals ask a lot of questions first. You should do the same. When you've determined their needs, explain enough about the product to get them excited about the features that interest them. Then communicate those features with advantages and benefits during a power presentation and demonstration. Learn to keep your customers involved with questions throughout the process. Don't make the mistake of telling them too much. You need their feedback, their agreement, and their buy-in. You accomplish this with a series of well-placed questions throughout the process. People are more excited when they are involved in the process - they feel more urgency and when they feel more urgency, they buy. After you do all of this professionally, closing is more of a formality. When you try to close before following these steps, closing is more like a brawl.

5

Stealth Selling Tactics–Your Competitive Edge

Which type of customer do you prefer working with, someone who already knows, likes and trusts you, or strangers? The answer is obvious. Repeat customers are easier to deal with, make the day brighter and make your job more fun. Since this is the case, what are you doing to turn today's sold customers into tomorrow's repeat buyers? Some salespeople build up a decent repeat and referral business in spite of themselves. People just plain like them and come back to buy. Since this is often the case, think of how much bigger a base of repeats and referrals you could build if you actually did it by design and had a plan to increase it every year. Statistically, loyal repeat buyers and referrals pay you more, shop others less and spread the word of your services to friends, family and co-workers adding even more business to your base. While many of them do so just because they like you, there are many more who do not go to much trouble to remember you. Most likely, you give them little reason to. Most shopping experiences are just like the last one and the one before that and the one before that. No one stands out. No one excels…just a bunch of average, ho-hum salespeople. What a *tremendous opportunity!* There couldn't be an easier profession to stand out in and to make a lasting impression! You'd have little competition! Everyone else is too busy being average and going through the motions! Today's buyers often have such low expectations of salespeople and their service that it leaves the door wide open for you to dominate. It all starts with the right attitude and the right plan. And since 99% of salespeople are "0 for 2" in those two categories, once you start off in the right direction, you'll leave the rest far behind.

The First Step In Stealth

The highest paid professionals in sales have built a successful base of repeat and referral customers. Often times these people don't work any harder or longer than the less successful salesperson. They just have a system. Follow-up and prospecting to increase your business takes a system. It takes organization and dedication. It takes daily work to maintain and build. That's why so few salespeople go to the trouble of doing it. Here are a few steps to get you started. Alter this as necessary to make it apply to your specific market.

1. **Begin a master list of contacts.** This should include all of your sold customers, working prospects, referrals, friends and acquaintances. Everyone you sell to, work a deal with, meet, etc., should go onto this list. The master list can be done on a database, in a file index card box or written in a notebook. It doesn't matter, just start your list. If you are new to the business, this will really be easy. If you've been at it a while and have hundreds or thousands of names, decide which you want on the list and get some secretarial help to compile them.

   Now that you have the list, decide what you will send and when you will send it. You may want to send thank you notes to everyone you talk to. A monthly or quarterly newsletter with updates about your product, holiday cards, etc. What you send is not as important as the fact that you send *something* and do it often. Follow-up and prospecting is the same as advertising. It works through repetition. Keep your mailers short and interesting. Don't get hung up on whether it's a literary work of art. **The idea is to get you in their door on a regular basis.** Send something at least every 45 days (eight times per year). Remember, people will not go to much trouble to remember you. The cure for this is repetition. Any solid follow-up system includes a balance of mail and phone calls. Don't depend strictly on the post office to maintain a relationship with your customer. They need to hear your voice. You need to hear their needs and concerns. You also have a better opportunity to uncover referrals on the phone than you do by mail. Set up a schedule to call your sold customers at least every 90 days (four times a year). It can be to check on their product, wish them a happy birthday or happy holiday, to advise them of items of interest concerning their purchase, etc. Get creative. Keep your calls short and to the point. Be friendly and remember **you are not**

calling to try and sell them anything on the phone. You're just staying in touch. Following this plan of mail and phone calls will compute to at least 12 contacts per year. This is called a "stealth" approach because your competitors and even the people you work with won't realize what you're doing to amass such a loyal customer base so quickly. The key is to be consistent and don't get too fancy.

2. **Organize what you want to send and say.** Keep it simple. Have your cards or letters printed up and sign them for a personal touch. Plan this out. Not only is it incredibly manageable, but the activity you create by doing so will create more activity and sales. If you have a "monster" base of business, enlist secretarial help to do the mailers and make the calls. Yes, it costs money. But not as much as it costs to keep losing customers and missing opportunities. Like so many other things vital to success in sales, follow-up and prospecting are things that will cost you some time and money. Don't make the mistake of getting so caught up with what it will cost to do it that you lose sight of the cost for not doing it. You can't begin to put a price on that.

Remember, stealth selling tactics get their name because your competition doesn't even know it's going on and neither will most of the people you work with. Your follow-up program is your secret weapon, your silent sales partner. What I've given you are very broad and general guidelines. Adapt them to your customer base and what you sell. Get organized. Get a system. Get busy. This is a long term cultivation process. It's like a snowball. It'll get bigger and bigger but *you've* got to get it rolling and keep it rolling.

6

Boot Camp For Millionaires

In sales, like life, there's a price to pay for success and you get exactly what you pay for. This can be good news or bad news, depending on the price you are paying or are willing to pay. Too many people think the price you pay is in terms of travel, stress, long hours, etc., and to some extent it is. But the most impacting price you can pay in sales is the price you pay to work on yourself, not on your job. ***Don't be one of those who waits around for things to get better***. This will only happen in the long term when you get better, and you can only get better by developing yourself. ***In short, you have to earn it!*** There are no shortcuts. It's common for salespeople to stop learning after their initial training period and years later they're still trying to advance a career with the skills they learned "once upon a time." They fail to seek out new information and get lulled into the warm comfort of routine called *mediocrity*. They quit learning so they quit growing and then wonder why their income, performance and prospects for the future have leveled off. It's vital to have a solid work ethic at your job. But what's more important is to have a solid and unrelenting work ethic when you work on your own development. When you stop just chasing money and first chase the skills, habits and attitudes needed to make more money a funny thing starts to happen; ***the money starts chasing you!*** When you focus more on what you are becoming, rather than what you are *getting*, you begin to get more. The problem is that most people get it backwards. They're chasing more and more money with entry level selling skills and inner motivation and wonder why they can't ever hit the big time. They'll catch up if and when their skills catch up. This is a simple, basic principle that salespeople unwittingly shortcut because they never put the effort forward to effectively plan their success, instead leaving it to chance.

Working on yourself is a daily thing. It has to be done incrementally, every day on good days and bad days, slow days and busy days. Some days you'll feel like it and some days you won't. You need self-discipline to keep pushing yourself during the times when you'd like to coast. One of the keys to success is developing the self-discipline to take complete and full control of yourself and your mind. This takes realigning your priorities. You can't wait and hope to *find* time to get better. You have to *make* time for improvement. In an earlier chapter on the daily budgeting of time to improve, selling skills, product skills, as well as attitude and motivation were identified as the three most vital areas to work on every day. It bears repeating that you will have to focus and *schedule* this time every day. Otherwise you'll never get around to it and it goes back on the shelf with the rest of your good intentions. Here is a sample plan on how you might begin your own "boot camp." Alter the suggestions where necessary to fit what you do and to fit your schedule:

1. When planning your day, list the activities you will work on for attitude and motivation, selling skills and product knowledge. Be specific. Write them in your planner. Look at theses daily exercises as a boot camp for millionaires. It takes focus, discipline and dedication, but you will be committing to what most of the population will not trouble themselves to do. This self-development will eventually cause you to think in different, bigger terms. Each day will be more exciting. Learning new things is motivating. We tend to forget that since we do it so seldom. This daily discipline will lead to higher levels of self-esteem and greater confidence than you ever had. Remember, you will be paying the price to improve your most valuable asset - *you!* You get what you pay for and, for perhaps the first time in a long time, you'll be sowing seeds for future harvests.

2. Start doing some of these activities as soon as you can once the day begins. If you can trade off your usual newspaper reading before you leave home and go over some selling scripts or read over some product brochures you have, do so. Turn your drive time into improvement time. Listen to a tape that will improve you instead of some R-rated deejay on a rock station. It's another trade off. Going to work on yourself early in the day gives you momentum. It gets the juices flowing and sets the tone for the whole day. Add up your drive time to and from work. If it is only 15 minutes each way, you get 2.5 hours of improvement every week, 10 hours each month and 120 hours per year - without working any longer or harder. You'll just be trading in mundane activities for new productive ones.

3. Once you are at work, and as the day progresses, use the time to complete the priorities you have left on your list. When you return home after work, don't go to bed until your self-improvement routine is complete. This is vital to committing to the habit of improvement. Yes, you may have to trade in some of your television time to complete your program for the day, but remember what Groucho Marx said, "I find television very educational. Every time someone turns it on I go read a book." Too many people waste all of their time watching other people live out their dreams on TV. They never get to develop and live out their own lives and dreams.

4. Read books. Some of your daily boot camp training should be spent reading books. There are literally hundreds of books on self-improvement, sales, management, leadership, thinking big, setting goals and the like. The sad fact is that the American Bookseller's Association says that seventy percent of Americans have not visited a book store in five years. They go on to say that fifty-eight percent of the population has not read a book since high school.

No wonder the country's such a mess! Not enough people are learning or growing and they end up resigned to an average life with average expectations and an average return. Most people don't read books or don't finish books because, like most everything else they do in life, they try to do it without a plan. They wing it. They have good intentions but no system. Yes, you should have a plan for reading a book. What gets planned gets done. If you haven't read a book in awhile, start out with reading one book per month. Does that sound like a lot? Let's break it down.

Buy a book you're interested in and take a look at how many pages it has. Let's say, for example, you find one that has 240 pages. Take the 240 pages and divide it by the number of days in the month. Let's say it's 30. Commit to reading eight pages per day, everyday and you'll finish your book. If you cannot see reading one book per month, can you see reading eight pages per day? The key is to set aside time each and every day to read the pages. As an alternative, you could decide to read an appropriate number of pages 4-5 days per week to finish the book.

Be creative and develop a plan that works for you. The key is to **develop a plan**–at least until your reading becomes a regular habit. I know people who easily read five books and more per month. Their daily reading assignment amounts to roughly 35-40 pages per day. Read half in the morning and half in the evening and you have the benefits and knowledge that five books per month (60 per year) can add to your abilities and your income. **Caution! The key is not to just get hung up on knowledge.**

Knowledge alone won't make you much money unless you take action and apply it.

Too many salespeople walk around with a wealth of knowledge between their ears and a wealth of emptiness in their wallets. IMPORTANT REMINDER: **Don't kid yourself into thinking you can achieve your boot camp activities after everything else is done.**

You need to plan your improvement activity as though it were an appointment. It is! It's an appointment with yourself. You owe some time and attention to yourself. You give yourself away for most of the day, so don't feel bad about scheduling appointments with yourself to improve. It's the only way it'll get done. You'll never find time to do it. It's like saving money. The most successful people who save money realize that they have to pay themselves *first*. They put money away for their savings as soon as they get their check because they know if they wait to save what's left over at the end of the month, there's never any extra! You need to pay yourself first. Think about this for a moment: To keep your car running right, you have regularly scheduled maintenance performed. Your pets get their shots when you get a notice from the vet that it's time to maintain their well-being. Chances are, you even take the time to get your clothing to the dry cleaners, pick it up and hang it with care in your closet. In light of this, would it be too much to ask yourself to give YOU some time each day devoted strictly to your self-development and financial well-being, and to make it a top priority? Isn't it at least as important as your car's oil, your dog, or your dirty clothes?

5. Get physical. No boot camp would be complete without going to work on the physical being. Regardless of what kind of shape you are in, small improvements in the physical arena reinforce the new mental and emotional health you're developing. There is no doubt that as you feel better, you work better. You have more energy, more self-esteem and more drive. The good news is that while you are developing the disciplines necessary to implement the principles in this book, physical disciplines can be developed more easily and simultaneously. Since going to work on yourself is an inside-out job, use the commitment and disciplines you have adopted to work on the "out" part as well. Get a check-up. Ask your doctor about improving your diet, taking vitamin or mineral supplements and an easy, gradual exercise routine. You can budget time to improve your health just as easily as improving the other skills we talked about. It will take the same commitment and focus and you'll have to make time for it. Once again, don't count on finding time. You've probably already been putting something like this off for too long. Maybe you've tried exercise or

better eating in the past and haven't been able to stick with it. So what! Take what you've learned from these past incidents and apply them to your new program to make sure it works this time. When you are working on self-development on the inside, you can accelerate to a higher speed and a higher plane if your body is more in tune with your mind. Make your physical well-being an ally on your climb to the next selling success level. Don't let it become a speed bump that keeps slowing you down and getting you off track.

6. Keep the "Big Picture" in mind during your training. You are working on yourself and it will have a positive effect on everything you do. You are *becoming* more and you will gain more. That's just the way it works. You are developing the power that comes with preparing and not reacting. Remember that whatever you do or don't do is a form of preparation. When you follow your boot camp routine, you are consciously preparing to succeed. When you do nothing, you are unconsciously preparing to fail. Remember that, either way, you *are* preparing for something. Most sales people never grasp this. Following your routine will prevent you from ever having to fake it. Joe Frazier said, "You can put together a fight plan or a life plan but when the action starts you're down to your reflexes. That's when the practice shows. If you cheated on your practice in the dark of the morning, you'll be found out under the bright lights."

You can use this daily self-development to improve every area of your life: personal, business, spiritual, mental, emotional, financial, etc. By going to boot camp, you can stop waiting to have a good day, week, month, year or career. You can start *making* them. In conclusion, as you read these daily doses for developing the right attitudes, skills and habits to rise and stay above the crowd, remember that your training and improvement regimen is not an *event*. It is an ongoing *process*. You are never trained, you are always training. The process is never completed, it's always ongoing.

Keeping this perspective and working on daily, incremental improvements will become more meaningful, and will have added impact for the rest of your career and your life. **In fact, it will become a way of life.**

7

How "Customization" Compounds Interest–And Sales

A common mistake of salespeople is to use the same canned, panned presentation and approach on all prospects. They try to take the customer and fit them into their style, rather than adjusting their sales style to fit the customer. Customizing your sales style to fit your customer compounds the interest a customer will have in doing business with you, and that in turn will compound your sales.

The four basic personality types have been examined ever since famed psychologist Carl Jung began his studies in the early 1900's. Understanding these types can give you an incredible edge in connecting with and selling your customers. It's up to you to determine which type you are dealing with and to customize your approach to that personality type. Doing this accomplishes several things:

1. It develops instant rapport with the prospect.

2. It removes the tension and conflict prevalent when the style and pace of salesperson and prospect clash.

3. It causes the salesperson to quickly connect with the prospect and causes the prospect to gain interest in doing business with the salesperson. After all, when people seem to be on the same page and speaking the same language, the atmosphere for mutual cooperation greatly multiplies and momentum is created.

Let's look at the four following sets of characteristics and begin the process of understanding the four basic personality types.

Pushers: This group likes to control things. They want to get to the bottom line and aren't interested in a lot of small talk. They fear that you'll waste their time. Pushers need to be convinced that you have respect for their wishes and concerns. They aren't the most loyal group of buyers in the world, often selling you out for a few bucks. However, the advantage to working with this group is that they are able to make decisions quickly so they can get on with other things. This group expects a salesperson to be professional and to "know his stuff." While they aren't interested in a bunch of technical details, they want a salesperson who knows the ropes and can get the deal done–quickly.

Tips for detecting Pushers: Pushers are likely to "cut to the chase" and want to get to the bottom line quickly. This means you may get pushed through the sales process without being able to explain the value and build rapport as completely as you like. They often let you know up front that they are shopping your competitors and are strictly looking for the best deal.

Tips for selling Pushers: Show respect for their time. Tell the Pusher that part of your job is to first make sure they are getting exactly what they want and then to present them with their options for owning it. Stay on track and to the point. Make the sales process efficient and hassle-free. Avoid frivolous small talk. While building rapport is more difficult, you will succeed by getting the Pusher to talk about himself, his job, hobbies and accomplishments.

Ponderers: This group likes information. Like **Pushers,** they are not as interested in a relationship with a salesperson as they are in getting the right product. They love to analyze–often to the point of paralyzing themselves into a state where they are unable to make a decision. They have to "think about it"–sometimes seemingly forever. They would rather discuss details than make small talk, and will be repulsed by a salesperson who they perceive as unprofessional or uninformed. This group often knows more about the product than the salesperson, so don't try to bluff them. Don't use exaggerated or general terms. Be precise and have the proof to back it up. Know that **Ponderers** fear making a mistake, and your best strategy is to remove the risk from the process. Trying to push them into a decision is disastrous. Don't challenge or argue with **Ponderers.** Instead, compliment their knowledge and research. Show that you want them to make the best decision and are willing to work with them until they feel they've reached that point.

Tips for detecting Ponderers. Ponderers have done their homework. They are in no hurry to make a decision and are not impulse buyers. They often ask technical questions to show off their knowledge and test yours. They get hung up on little details. They are mostly reserved and introverted.

Tips for selling Ponderers. A Ponderer's biggest fear is making a mistake. Provide plenty of information for them to evaluate and keep them focused on the big picture when they tend to get hung up on little things. Tell them that part of your job is to stop them from making a mistake and to provide the best information to allow them to make a sound decision. They are favorably influenced by trial periods or guarantees that remove risk from the process. As with the Pusher, avoid frivolous small talk. Stay on track. Compliment them on their knowledge and research. Remark that by doing their homework they are in a much better position to make a decision than ninety percent of your customers.

Partners: This group is interested in a relationship with a salesperson and the salesperson's company. They want to feel comfortable with you and know that you'll be there for them after the sale. They are interested in referrals who can speak well of doing business with you. Take the time to ask them plenty of questions so they feel that you completely understand their wants and needs. Trying to rush this group will be a turn-off. Learn to sell this group and you will build the ultimate customers for life. These people are your most loyal customers.

Tips for detecting Partners: Unlike Pushers and Ponderers, Partners are relationship oriented. They are as interested in you and your company as they are your product. They ask questions about service after the sale and want to feel that they will be well taken care of during and after the sale. They may mention that friends or relatives purchased your product/service, as they are swayed heavily by testimonials.

Tips for selling Partners: Sell yourself first and foremost, then your company, then your product/service. Talk in terms of long-term relationships with your customers and service after the sale. Mention the number of repeat buyers and referrals you get. Provide testimonials if you have them. Introduce them to as many other nice people in your organization as you can. Make them feel part of the family. Let them know that you are personally available and very accessible after the sale for problems and questions.

Players: This group wants to be your buddy. They want to be liked and will work as hard to build rapport as you do. They are not into details or long processes. Players are an impulsive group and very subject to emotional selling and mental ownership. They get bored easily, so keep things moving. They will talk all day if you let them, so work hard to keep things on track. This is the most fun group to work with. If you are timid, or a stick-in-the-mud, you'll have to loosen up and have some fun if you want to sell Players.

How to detect Players: Players love to socialize. They are as interested in building rapport with you as you are with them. They want you to like and accept them. They are visual people who like the way things look. In their exuberance in having an audience—you—they are prone to digress and speak on a variety of subjects. Like Partners, Players are very relationship oriented.

How to sell Players: Don't bore them with details and too much information. Resist the temptation to get right to the bottom line. They want to have fun first. Loosen up and be genuinely interested in them and their stories. Talk in emotional terms: how great something will look or feel, what their friends will think, etc. Take advantage of their impulsive tendencies by making sure they get a feel for the product/service. Get them involved in the process. If you are selling a product, make sure they are an active part of the demonstration.

Keep in mind that there is not one right or wrong group. The key technique to customization is to quickly identify which type you are working with and adjust your approach to fit the prospect. Most people are combinations of the four groups, but one will usually dominate.

It is also important to identify which group you belong to. Can you see potential problems if you are a **Pusher** and try to deal with a **Ponderer** without altering your approach? How about the opposite scenario? Can you see the trouble with a **Player** not adjusting to the pace of a **Partner, Ponderer or Pusher?** Failing to make the necessary adjustments is precisely why so many sales are missed; most salespeople never really know why. People buy from those they believe to be honest, are comfortable with and see value in. They buy from salespeople who match well with them and who remove the tension and conflict from the process. All things being equal, people buy from people they like. Trying to fit the customer into your style is foolish and shortsighted. *You* must make the adjustments, not your prospect. *You* must customize your approach to fit the customer. Once you connect with a customer, you develop a tremendous edge.

Think about this: If you never alter your style and pace to match your customer, statistically you will only be connecting with one out of four prospects. By customizing, you can literally quadruple your chances of making the sale! You will have an opportunity to connect with four out of four customers, instead of just one. Does this mean you'll sell everybody? Of course not, but by connecting with virtually everyone you talk to, rather than potentially turning off the three out of four customers who do not match your type, your sales can't help but multiply exponentially!

8

Getting Ready For The Climb

You can begin the daily strategies on any day of the year. They are in a balanced order, encompassing all areas of skills, habits and attitudes. Read them carefully and skip back to previous passages you highlighted to read again for reinforcement.

Reread the initial seven chapters again throughout the year. **Complete the Action Plans twice per month. Follow through!** Repetition, reinforcement, application and reflection are the keys to incorporating the strategies in this book. Use them to soar above the crowd.

Read each entry early in the day; preferably before you begin work. Think about how it applies to you. Jot down the main idea and refer to it during work. Make it the "strategy of the day." Be patient with yourself. Remember that the process of improvement never ends. Taking time to work on yourself is the best time you can spend. So read the daily strategy, apply it, reinforce it and internalize it during the day and then reflect on it when your work is through. Very soon you'll notice the impact that consistent, ongoing improvement will have on your outlook, performance, income, career advancement and your life overall. You'll see what it's like to *Sell Above The Crowd.* You can't coast there, you have to climb. So let's get started *Selling Above The Crowd!*

Skill, Habit and Attitude Targets For Improvement

Before beginning the daily strategies, write down the primary skill, habit and attitude you have that you consider your weakest area. Keep this area in mind as you proceed through the strategies, then return to this page and record ways you've found to improve these areas. Make copies of this page and continue to add to your skill targets as the year progresses:

The number one skill area I need to improve is:

Using the following strategies I can improve this area immediately:

The number one habit I need to improve is:

Using the following strategies I can improve this area immediately:

The number one attitude problem I have is:

Using the following strategies I can improve this area immediately:

---

365 Strategies For Sales Excellence

JANUARY 1

Have you planned out the specific steps you need to follow this year to become more successful, or are you going to leave your improvement to chance? Map out which selling, product, and attitude and motivational skills you want to develop this year and commit to a plan to get it done (refer to Chapter 3). The more you plan, the more you'll improve; the more you improve, the more you'll earn. Be specific and break your plan for skill development into monthly, weekly, and daily objectives. Commit to spend the year growing at an incrementally consistent pace. When you plan for improvement, you plan for success. After all, how many top performers have you ever heard say, "I just made it up as I went along?" Start or update your plan for progress today. It's the first step above the crowd.

Action I will take today: _____

_____

JANUARY 2

In order to develop the skills necessary to take you to the next level in your career you're going to need resources: books, tapes and videos. Don't wait for your company to provide you with the tools for success. Invest in yourself. Start slowly and stay consistent. Focusing on skill development keeps you out of ruts and prevents you, your attitude and your career from getting stale or leveling off. Go to a bookstore today and begin–or add to your own personal development library. Upgrade your resources constantly. Combine tapes with books or videos.

These tools stimulate your thinking, reinforce your development and make each day a little bit more exciting.

Today I will: _____

_____

JANUARY 3

Want to get better at closing right now? As you study and practice closing techniques and methods for overcoming objections, remember this; no words, scripts or tricky phrases are going to be very effective if your customer doesn't like or trust you. Closing won't bail you out of a bad first impression, a weak meet and greet, a lousy investigation or a slipshod presentation. Most salespeople never grasp the importance of this. Practice *slowing the process down* **today.** Be enthusiastic with everyone and take the time to build rapport and relationships. It's an investment in time and energy that pays big dividends when it comes time to wrap up the sale. Don't get into such a hurry to close that you neglect to build the foundation you'll need.

Strategy I will use today: _____

_____

JANUARY 4

Step up the enthusiasm today and stop "going through the motions" with your customers. Transfer a genuine concern for their needs and your excitement for your product to them and watch your sales take off. Put fun and enthusiasm back into your work ethic. People buy when they feel positive about you and your product. Use enthusiasm to create this state for your customers. Remember what Vince Lombardi said, "If you're not fired with enthusiasm, you'll be fired with enthusiasm." Interesting choice, isn't it?

Action I will take today: _____

_____

JANUARY 5

Don't tell them everything you know! Give out product information selectively. It's important to know everything about your product, but don't dump all of that on each customer. Find their buying motives or "hot buttons" and talk about those things which excite and interest your customer. Every one of the hot button features you talk about moves the prospect closer to the sale. Everything else you tell them can push them further away. People buy when they are excited, not when they are confused and overloaded with too much information. Practice "selective" presentations today.

Today I will: _____

_____

JANUARY 6

When you're with a customer, are you asking or answering most of the questions? Remember, whoever is *asking* most of the questions is in control. Questions give you an opportunity to discover wants and needs, gain minor agreements and control the sale into a closing opportunity. If you are just giving out information, remember that you can't tell your way into a sale–you have to *ask* your way to it. Questions give you control of the process. Think about effective questions that you can begin to use to add value, gain agreement and move your customers closer to the sale.

Strategy I will use today:_____

_____

JANUARY 7

Have you tried anything new lately? Any new prospecting or closing methods? Any different approaches for presenting your product? You should always be on the lookout for better ways of doing what you do. It's the best way to avoid ruts. Go out on a limb. That's where the fruit can be found. Think about some of the phrases or methods you've been using lately for presenting, prospecting, overcoming objections and closing. Is it time to change or polish your approach? Make today the day you try something new and move out of that old comfort zone.

Action I will take today: _____

_____

JANUARY 8

Most of us don't try new things because we're afraid of failing and falling. Failing and falling is fine as long as you learn something on the way back up. Let failure be your teacher, not your undertaker. In fact, if you haven't been making any mistakes lately, it's a sign you're playing it too safe. Think of the last failure or mistake you made. What did you learn? How will that make you better? Use that information to improve your approach. As Henry Ford said, "Failure is the opportunity to begin again more intelligently." Commit to learning from failure–not beating yourself up because of it.

Today I will: _____

_____

JANUARY 9

If you should get rejected by a client today, how will you handle it? Just as with failure, you can't let rejection send you flying backwards. Salespeople tend to take rejection too personally. Realize that most often it is not you being rejected, but your price, product, company, etc. Focus on doing a better job of selling yourself, and it'll be tougher for the client to reject your product. Think about the last few deals you were told "no" on. Send the clients a note of thanks for their time. Call them from time to time and keep them updated on inventories, market conditions, etc. By keeping an apparently "dead" relationship going, you do a convincing job of selling yourself. **Turn rejection into a challenge to be met, not a sentence to be served.** Revive contact with these "dead" deals today. You'll be planting seeds for tomorrow's success as well as cultivating powerful habits and ethics for your journey above the crowd.

Strategy I will use today: _____

_____

JANUARY 10

Who do you associate with at work, the most or least productive salespeople? Too many average salespeople flock together to share one another's misery. They stand around in huddles discussing management's sins and massaging one another's egos. Watch the associations you have where you work because that's precisely where you are headed. Take an objective view of your associates today. Are they advancing or slowing down your climb? Are they inspirations or "grave diggers"? Be honest with yourself and take the personalities out of the equation. Decide whom you may have to walk away from, or at least put some distance between, in order to focus on being more productive and positive.

Action I will take today: _____

_____

JANUARY 11

Don't try to get ahead in sales strictly by working harder and longer. The key to long term success in sales is learning to work *smarter.* Commit today to plan and then fill your days with selling activities so that you're doing something at every moment that will either lead to a sale today or sometime in the future. Focus on making something happen and stop waiting for it to fall in your lap. Create your own activity by working smarter as well as harder. What specific selling activities can you begin to plan into your day that will produce more results? Start them today!

Today I will: _____

JANUARY 12

Have you fallen into the warm comfort of routine during your daily activities? Are you in a rut or stuck in a comfort zone? Following the plan you put together at the start of the program will keep you focused on incremental improvement and skill development. You have to keep moving. Pinpoint the areas in your day where you have fallen prey to the warm comfort of routine. If the plan you put together isn't doing enough to address them, change course now so that they are eliminated. Comfort zones can turn into dead zones. Diligently following a plan for success will put you in the end zone. Pick which zone you want to be in today.

Strategy I will use today:_____

JANUARY 13

When you look at where you are in sales for the month or the level at which you are at in your career overall, remember one thing: Where you are is not as important as the direction you are *headed.* If you are doing very well but don't have a plan to keep moving in the right direction, you're headed for trouble. If you're not where you want to be yet, but are moving toward that place, your future is brightening. So where are you? And more importantly, what do you have in place to move you in the right direction? Ask yourself this question today and regularly for the rest of your career. It increases focus and helps avoid complacency.

Action I will take today: _____

JANUARY 14

Take a look at your priorities today. They should include developing the skills we talked about for selling, product knowledge and attitude and motivation. They should also include the selling activities you designated with which to fill your day. Remember this: *Priorities must be scheduled. You can't wait until you find time to get them done.* Start putting priorities onto your schedule today just like you would any other appointment. Treat priorities with the same respect and regard you would an appointment with a customer. If something comes up in the day to get your priorities off track, just reschedule it. The key is to focus on priorities by *making* time to complete them–not waiting to find the time.

Today I will: _____

_____

JANUARY 15

Be patient with your progress. You don't have to go from zero to hero overnight. Whether you improve 100% in a given area or 1% in 100 different areas, it still comes out to 100% improvement. Again, the important thing is to develop the self-discipline to improve incrementally *every* day. Success has been described as coming in fourth place, exhausted but excited because you came in fifth last time. Keep improvement in perspective. What improvements have you made the past few days that you may have taken for granted? Realize that each improvement is an important step to where you want to go. They are *all* significant. Decide today to do a better job of recognizing each improvement as such and acknowledging the progress you are making. Use these minor improvements to build your own self-esteem and confidence.

Strategy I will use today:_____

_____

JANUARY
MID-MONTH ACTION PLAN

_____

_____

_____

_____

_____

_____

_____

_____

JANUARY 16

If you want to work smarter each day, and not necessarily longer and harder, and if you want to budget time to improve on a daily basis, you will need to plan your day. Plan tomorrow tonight before you go home. Come in tomorrow with a firm plan and focus–a blueprint. If you wait until you come in tomorrow to try to plan the day, you are subject to interruptions, phone calls, meetings and dozens of other distractions that prevent you from completing your plan. Get a planner. Then, to get the most out of each day, plan it *before* you start it, at night before you go home. Start this strategy today and watch the momentum you build when you come in tomorrow.

Action I will take today: _____

_____

JANUARY 17

Think of all the successful people you know or have known. How many ever told you, "I just made it up as I went along?" Successful people plan. They don't come into work with a lottery mindset, hoping today is the day their number comes up. It has been estimated that one hour of planning saves three hours of execution time. If you don't take the time to shape your day, you'll be *shaped* by the circumstances that arise during your day. As part of yesterday's strategy, you planned today before you went home. Tonight when you plan tomorrow's work, be more specific. Learn what worked today and what did not. Incorporate the improved adjustments daily.

Today I will: _____

_____

January 18

When do your customers buy; when they are excited or when they're bored? What are you doing when presenting the product to get them more excited? Don't just present features. Features raise the cost of owning the product. Explain the feature as well as the advantage (what the feature does) and the benefit (what it means to the customer). Feature, advantage, benefit presentations; all build the value of owning the product. Your customers are more likely to buy *now* and to pay more when they see more value than *cost*. Take your best selling product and think about three of the most common features you point out to customers. Then think about what the advantages and benefits are so you can expand your next presentation to build more value.

Strategy I will use today:_____

_____

January 19

What are you afraid of? George Patton said, "Fear kills more often than death." Death just kills you once. Fear can kill you over and over, day after day. Are there certain types of customers or objections you are afraid of? Guess what. They're not going away so you might as well learn to handle them. Write down the top three or four objection or rejection scenarios you fear most. Put a plan together for what you'll say and do the next time they come up. Then practice, drill and rehearse these scenarios until you have replaced fear with confidence. Remember, repetition beats adversity and preparation reduces stress. Preparation today makes your job easier tomorrow.

Action I will take today: _____

_____

January 20

You know the great thing about sales? There are dozens of ways to get better. There's not just one narrow path you have to stay on to succeed. You can improve your skills in presenting, closing, overcoming objections, prospecting, follow-up, telephone skills, building rapport, investigating wants and needs, setting goals, planning your day, getting referrals, product knowledge and so on. The really good news is that it doesn't take all of these things to make a positive difference in what we do. Some of us are just a close away from the next level in our careers. Some are a follow-up system, a prospecting system or some product knowledge away from making improvements which will take us to the next level. Which area are you working on today?

Today I will: _____

_____

JANUARY 21

Do you stay in contact with the people you sell? Do you prefer working with repeat customers who know, like and trust you, or are you happier trying to sell strangers who don't know you or like you yet? *Don't count on your employer to maintain relationships with your customers.* That's your primary responsibility. Set up a follow-up system to maintain the relationships you've started. If you do this, you'll have less competition. You will be a stand out. Repeat customers are the bread and butter of the top earners in sales. The top earners aren't necessarily smarter, they just have a system. Set up your own. Decide what you want to send, when you want to call and what you'll say when you do. The key to follow-up is repetition. People won't go to much trouble to remember you, so start planning your system today.

Strategy I will use today: _____

_____

JANUARY 22

Can you take it? When you receive criticism or feedback from the people you work with or from your boss, do you jump to your own defense? Next time it happens, try listening and evaluating before you summarily brush it off. Feedback gives us an opportunity to grow. John Wooden said, "It's what you learn after you know it all that counts." If the criticism isn't valid then don't worry about it, but at least give it a chance to help you improve. Focus on this today.

Action I will take today: _____

_____

JANUARY 23

Stop giving up so easily. The National Sales Executive Association estimates that 48% of salespeople quit calling after one unsuccessful call. Twenty-five percent quit calling after the second call. Another twelve percent quit after the third call. Only ten percent keep calling. No wonder it's estimated that 20% of the salespeople earn 80% of the commissions. Pull out the last couple of deals you've given up on. Make the extra calls to revive those deals today; then get in the habit of extending your normal follow-up time frame. **Make today the day you become the 1 in 10 who keeps calling!**

Today I will: _____

_____

JANUARY 24

To stop quitting takes persistence. Rich de Vos said, "Persistence is stubbornness with a purpose." Persistence can wear down resistance. Too many salespeople stop one or two attempts short of the sale. What a shame! To be persistent, you'll need more tools to persist with (closing questions, overcoming objection techniques, etc). Be creative and always have something new each time you try to make another attempt at a sale. As long as you bring something new to the table, it's difficult for your prospect to be annoyed at your persistence. As you develop your skills and turn them into action, you cannot help but become more persistent. They go hand in hand. Need more persistence? Get more skills! We've talked about persistence the past couple of days. If you haven't already, it's time to commit to slow down and work the deals you are on more completely. Take the long-term, tenacious approach. Persistence does wear down resistance. Resist the temptation to rush into a new deal because the grass looks greener. Yes, it's okay to go into new deals. No, it's not okay to do so at the expense of the tough ones you are already invested in.

Strategy I will use today: _____

_____

JANUARY 25

Do you like what you do? Ever think about changing jobs or companies? Before you do, take a look at yourself. Sometimes you think you need a change of scenery when all you need is a change of self. If the problem is with you, it'll still be with you regardless of what you do or where you go. In the areas of product knowledge and selling skills, attitude and motivation, where is the biggest area in which you could use a change of self? Today, make sure you are addressing these areas in your daily plan and goals.

Action I will take today: _____

_____

JANUARY 26

What happens when you have an unhappy customer? When you lose a sale? When you have a confrontation with your boss? Do you consider these as problems? They're not. They're just conditions of being in sales and dealing with people. So stop letting these things throw you off track and getting your attitude out of whack. As author John Maxwell says, "Your problems aren't your problem. How your problems affect you–your attitude–is your problem. Fix that and your problems are no problem." Resolve today to take the "problems" that arise and make a more conscious effort to choose a more productive response. Make this a habit.

Today I will: _____

_____

JANUARY 27

Does your boss think you are a whiner or a winner? Whiners bring the problems they find to their boss and make sure they are aware of them. Winners bring the problems they find to their boss with suggested solutions. Big difference isn't there? Think about the last few areas in your job and in your company that you brought to a supervisor's attention. Did you also bring possible solutions? Start to see things from the Winner vs. Whiner perspective today. It will help you handle situations more productively.

Strategy I will use today:_____

_____

JANUARY 28

Do you have a "fair weather attitude?" Do you have fair weather enthusiasm? Anyone can be enthusiastic and positive when things are going well. How do you act when they're not going so well? The math on this one is easy. Bad attitude costs you bundles of big money; good attitude grants you great gains. As Winston Churchill said, "Success is going from failure to failure without loss of enthusiasm." Have an all weather attitude and *all* weather enthusiasm. Make today the day you begin carrying your own weather around within you.

Action I will take today: _____

_____

JANUARY 29

Where are you? It doesn't matter. It's where you finish that counts. Tom Landry, Chuck Noll and Bill Walsh coached NFL teams to nine of fifteen Superbowl victories between 1974 and 1989. They also had three of the worst first season win-loss records in NFL history. They developed and followed a plan to change the scenery from the outhouse to the penthouse. How's your plan coming along? Are you working it or is it on the back shelf with the rest of the good intentions? Check your momentum today. Fine tune where necessary.

Today I will: _____

_____

JANUARY 30

Are you treating everyone like a buyer? When was the last time you guessed wrong? How much did it cost you? Prequalifying kills your career on the installment plan; one judgement at a time See and treat everyone as a qualified buyer until they prove they are not. It's easy to find reasons not to. The harder–and more profitable–road is to stay on track with each and every customer. This consistency builds powerful habits. Focus on this mentality this week. Catch yourself when you get off track.

Strategy I will use today:_____

_____

JANUARY 31

Run the roadblock. Don't let your errors or the errors of others get you off track and don't stop when a roadblock appears. Conrad Hilton said, "Successful people keep moving. They make mistakes but they don't quit." What hurdles have slowed you down recently? Do you have any momentum in these areas today? Regroup around these challenges and jump-start your commitment to overcoming them. When roadblocks come up, run the roadblock!

Action I will take today: _____

_____

JANUARY
MONTH-END ACTION PLAN

_____

_____

_____

_____

_____

_____

_____

_____

_____

_____

_____

_____

_____

FEBRUARY 1

Focus on today. Stop talking about what's going to happen tomorrow, next week or next month. John Wooden said, "Make today your masterpiece." There's no reason today can't be the best day of your career. Stop thinking your best days are out there somewhere. They're right in front of you. What can you do today that will help make it a masterpiece? Stop letting the days slip by. They are in limited supply. If you don't treat today like it has the potential to be a masterpiece, chances are that it won't.

Action I will take today: _____

_____

FEBRUARY 2

Today isn't practice. Too often we tend to treat what's happening like it's a dress rehearsal. We take tomorrow for granted and don't get the most out of today. We don't get a moment of time back, much less a week. So, think about today. Are you prepared to get the most out of today? Do you have a proactive plan to *make* something happen, or are you willing to *wait* for something to happen to you? If so, do you think that what "just happens" is likely to be what you want it to be? Spend some time right now and reflect on a couple of the deals you worked recently. What did you learn? What would you do differently today if you had the same opportunities? Focus on the differences and be ready with your new approach as similar opportunities arise today.

Today I will: _____

_____

FEBRUARY 3

Quit cheating yourself. If you're quicker to drop the price of your product than you are to justify it, you're getting it backward. Dropping the price should be your last resort, not your first option when negotiation sets in. Learn to build enough value to *justify* the price and master the words and phrases that will allow you to do so convincingly. Remember, when you drop the price, you drop your commission at the same time. What words can you polish up today that will allow you to antici-pate situations where you will have an opportunity to either justify the price or drop it? If you don't have the words to justify, dropping the price is your alternative. Remember, most deals are missed by a few words, not a few dollars.

Strategy I will use today: _____

_____

FEBRUARY 4

Knowledge alone isn't worth much by itself. When you learn more about your product, attend training sessions, watch training tapes, etc. does your learning turn into *knowledge* or *action?* Filling your head with knowledge isn't enough. It only produces income when you turn it into action. You wouldn't expect to learn to skydive by taking a correspondence course in your home. You'd have to get out and get involved with it, experience it and take action. You can't effectively use the information you learn about selling without putting it to use, either. When you leave the knowledge in your head, you leave money on the table as well. What knowledge are you walking around with that you could turn into action? Make it pay starting today!

Action I will take today: _____

FEBRUARY 5

You have two new jobs. The first one is to prevent your customers from making a mistake. You have to be convinced that if they buy another product or purchase from another salesperson that they are making a mistake. Your second job is to make the purchase make sense. Help your customers justify the money they are trading for your product. When they are spending more than they had planned, help them rationalize it by motivating them to feel that they are doing the right thing and be able to show them why they are. Keep your two jobs in perspective with the next customer you are with and remember what Zig Ziglar said: "You can have everything you want in life if you will just help enough other people get what they want."

Today I will: _____

FEBRUARY 6

Are you motivated today? Does your boss motivate you? You are ultimately responsible for your own inner motivation. External motivation from others is important and gratifying but most often it's just a short burst of ceremony that wears off quickly. To be successful over the long term, your motivation must come from the inside out, not the outside in. You must internalize it. Attitude and motivation is something you should work on daily. Develop it just as you would a product or selling skill. It's the fuel for everything else positive and productive that you do. Have you been getting enough of your motivation from the right place, or have you been depending on outside sources that you can't control? Starting today, focus on getting your drive from the one area you can control–yourself!

Strategy I will use today: _____

_____

FEBRUARY 7

Do the little things. Do you set goals, plan your day, develop your selling, product knowledge and attitude skills, practice drilling and rehearsing daily? These tasks are time consuming and require discipline and hard work. Most people don't go to the trouble to do them. Author E.M. Gray wrote, "Successful people make the habit of doing things failures don't like to do. Successful people don't like to do them, either, but they subordinate their dislike to the strength of their purpose." Successful people force themselves to do the little things so that they can achieve the big things they so badly desire. Have you been forcing yourself to do enough of these things daily? What extra little things are you going to do today that set you above the crowd?

Action I will take today: _____

_____

FEBRUARY 8

When do you improve? You rarely develop any new closing, presentation or overcoming objection skills when you are with a customer. In fact, when you are with a customer, you have to play whatever hand you are holding as far as the skill levels you possess. It's what you do *in between* customers that makes you better. This is when you put your hand together. This is where you either drink coffee and gossip, or practice a close, listen to a motivational tape or study your product. What you do to put your hand together will determine whether you are holding any aces or will have to fold when it comes time to play that hand with the next customer.

Today I will: _____

_____

FEBRUARY 9

Get uncomfortable. Too much comfort breeds complacency. It closes your mind to new ideas. It makes you afraid to change or try new things. Push yourself out of your comfort zone on a daily basis. Post a sign in your office or on your notebook that says, "Am I doing the most productive thing right now?" J.F.K. said, "There are risks and costs to any program of action but they are far less than the long term costs of comfortable inaction." Look at your daily routine. What patterns of "comfortable inaction" can you break out of today?

Strategy I will use today: _____

_____

FEBRUARY 10

When do you decide to take action and prospect for new customers? Do you wait for something bad to happen before you are prompted to put a plan together? Does it take a couple of down months to force you into putting a prospecting plan together? Remember, Noah didn't wait until it was raining to start building the ark. Continually evaluate and follow your plan to take you to the next level, in good times or bad. There is no season to get busy and get better. It's a year-round project.

Action I will take today: _____

_____

FEBRUARY 11

Don't allow the pat you give yourself on the back to become a massage. Instead, just give it a quick tap. Too many salespeople let up after a big month or a big quarter. Remember that anyone can be great for a day, a week, a month or a year. Professionals continue to stay the course and focus on improving their vital skill areas, even when things are going well. They don't relax or let up. Like Will Rogers said, "Even if you're on the right track you'll get run over if you just sit there." What will you do after your next big month to keep the momentum going?

Today I will: _____

_____

FEBRUARY 12

Avoid the crowds. Zig Ziglar said that if you go the second mile there won't be as much traffic there. It's less crowded. You know where it's crowded? It's crowded at the bottom. The selling profession produces a huge "mass of average." Avoid the crowds. What can you do with your next sales opportunity to go the second mile? Then think about how you can go the extra mile for an entire day, week, month, quarter and year. Have you spent enough time on the second mile lately? What more can you do beginning today?

Strategy I will use today: _____

_____

FEBRUARY 13

When do you change? Author John Maxwell said that there are three times when people change: When they learn enough to where they'll want to. When they receive enough to where they'll be able to. Or when they hurt enough to where they have to. If you'll make the effort to learn enough about your business, and if you receive enough help and coaching to implement what you learn and make the changes you want, you'll never have to worry about hurting enough to where you have to change. What are the last couple of major changes you had to make in your career? Which of the three scenarios prompted the change? Change is inevitable. How you do it is up to you.

Action I will take today: _____

_____

FEBRUARY 14

Shut up! Too many salespeople forget one of the most basic laws of selling: after you ask a closing question, shut up! The next one who talks loses. Have you been talking past the sale? Have you been asking closing questions at the right time? Have you been asking the right type of closing questions - one that provides an either/or alternative to buying your product instead of a "yes" or "no" take it or leave it proposition? Don't ask "yes" or "no" closing questions. The customer has a 50/50 chance of making the wrong choice. Ask either/or closing questions instead. Then shut up long enough to give your customer a chance to pick the best option and consummate the deal.

Today I will: _____

_____

Selling Above The Crowd

FEBRUARY 15

What do you do in your "drive-time"? Listen to motivational tapes and selling tapes while driving back and forth to work. Keep yourself tuned-up and sharp. Add up the hours you spend commuting each week and you'll see the potential to get the equivalent of a degree in selling and motivation during time that you normally waste. What will help you have more fun and make more money; dulling your senses by listening to an "R" rated Rock & Roll deejay or feeding your mind with the power you need to fuel improvement in your career and your life? If you haven't by now, start your "drive-time" education today. It's your personal and competitive edge.

Strategy I will use today: _____

FEBRUARY
MID-MONTH ACTION PLAN

_____

_____

_____

_____

_____

_____

_____

FEBRUARY 16

When you are hired for a sales position, does that *make* you a salesperson or does it give you the opportunity to *become* one? You *become* a salesperson and then a sales professional when you develop the skills, habits and attitudes to take control of a sale, build rapport and value and close the deal. Until then you are a salesperson on paper–little more than a well-intentioned greeter. What you have *become* is your competitive advantage over the other sales people in your company and/or industry. Do a quick inventory of your competitive advantages. What do you do that gives you an edge over your competitors? What do you know that gives you an edge? More importantly, what are you currently working on to increase that advantage? Review your competitive advantages on a regular basis.

Action I will take today: _____

_____

FEBRUARY 17

Go to work to work. How many hours do you spend at work actually doing something directly related to creating a sale? On average, salespeople spend around one-third of their day performing productive activities that will lead to a sale. The rest of the time is normally spent visiting and waiting around for something to happen. Too many salespeople go to work without focus. It starts with a day and soon ends up turning into a career of waiting. When you plan your day and develop the skills and attitudes that enable you to fill your day with selling activities that lead to a sale now or somewhere down the road, you are taking the first step away from the "pack" and into the pros. Take an inventory of your average day right now. How many hours are you really spending creating sales? Where can you improve?

Today I will: _____

_____

FEBRUARY 18

Are you a goal setter? Studies show that only three percent of the population set goals the right way. Goals set right are written down, with a deadline and a written plan on how the goal will be reached. Too many salespeople have goals in their heads. When you write it down you are beginning the first serious step toward commitment to the goal. A deadline firms it up even more and a written plan makes it real. It's what gets you there. Goals are really a dime a dozen. Specific, step-by-step plans are where the money's at. Are your goals on paper or in your head? Are you really a goal setter or just the king of wishful thinking? Do a self-assessment on your status as a goal setter. Where can you improve? Take action today in this area!

Strategy I will use today: _____

_____

FEBRUARY 19

Just walk away. When others start their tirades and critiques of everything wrong at work, just walk away. These negative conversations start and stop numerous times during any given day. They accomplish nothing. They destroy attitudes and morale. Will listening to these conversations help motivate you? Will they improve your attitude? Will they move you towards your goals? Use these conversations as your cue to exit. As Calvin Coolidge said, "Cynics don't create." When others start tearing down, go create something positive, like a sale. This takes discipline and conscious effort. Today, begin paying closer attention to these types of situations and use them as a cue to go do something productive. Become more aware of what—and who—you are listening to.

Action I will take today: _____

_____

FEBRUARY 20

Quit counter-punching and take control. Too many salespeople go into the sales process with a customer adopting a counter-punch mentality. We wait to react to what the customer says and does. They punch, we counter-punch. They say this, we say that. Take control! The customer will respond to you. Take the offensive. Remember that it's the offense that takes you into the end-zone 99% of the time. Focus on positive control today.

Today I will: _____

_____

FEBRUARY 21

Make goals real. Realistic and achievable are two key words in the goals you set. Give serious thought to where you want to be. Factor in possible roadblocks and bumps along the way. Then set a goal that you can believe in and that will cause you to stretch. Don't psych yourself out with "highball" goals that look good on paper but defeat you before you start. Goals should be motivating, not intimidating. Are yours? Take a look at your goals and assess whether you feel they are realistic or not.

Strategy I will use today: _____

_____

FEBRUARY 22

Concentration and elimination. What do your goals cause you to do? No goal or plan is worth the paper it's written on unless it starts you doing something. That's the purpose of a plan to go with the goal - *action!* Evaluate your daily time and determine if the way you spend your time moves you toward your goals. Your plan should help bring out the principles of concentration and elimination. Goals and plans should create concentration toward what you want and elimination of activities that hinder your success. Are your goals moving you toward this end? If they aren't, either the goal is lame or your effort is lacking. Decide which is the case today and fix it.

Action I will take today: _____

_____

FEBRUARY 23

Don't let yourself off the hook. When you set realistic and achievable goals and put a solid plan together to get you there, stick with it. Don't give yourself reasons for not hitting it when unexpected events come up to throw you off track. These should be factored into the goals you set. No loopholes, no options for failure. Remember, concentration and elimination. Think about the last time or two you relieved yourself of responsibility for not hitting a goal. How did it really make you feel? Resolve not to let it happen again.

Today I will: _____

_____

FEBRUARY 24

Leave the goal alone. If you do hit a solid series of stumbling blocks that throws you so far off track that your goal seems out of reach, leave the goal alone. First, re-look at the plan you put together to get you there. Is it still viable? Is it realistic and effective? Does it cause you to take the right action? Setting a goal is worth about 25% of the effectiveness in hitting it. The other 75% comes from the day to day effort and work that comes from following the plan. Look at the plan first.

Strategy I will use today: _____

_____

FEBRUARY 25

Review. You move towards what you think about. The more you review your goals and focus on them, the quicker you'll get there. Too many salespeople set their goals and then set them on the back shelf and forget about them. They are out of sight and literally out of mind. Reviewing your goals should become part of your daily attitude and motivational training. Review, focus, work, achieve. Make time to review today and turn it into a daily habit. You can't afford to be without the focus this discipline will bring you.

Action I will take today: _____

FEBRUARY 26

Pay yourself. After you set a long-term goal, your plan should include a number of short-term goals to be accomplished on the way to the main goal. As you achieve the short-term goals, reward yourself. Know in advance that when you get to point A , you'll reward yourself with something. When you get to point B, give yourself something else. Your rewards could be as simple as a night out or a weekend away or as extravagant as you'd like to make them. Goal setting should be fun. Write down a series of rewards to go along with your goals. The journey should be just as much fun and just as rewarding as reaching the destination. Don't turn it into a death march. Set some rewards for yourself today.

Today I will: _____

FEBRUARY 27

Get inside help. Normally, everyone sets a number of "outside" goals: money, position, possessions, vacations, etc. Set inside goals to help you reach the outside goals. Do you need to develop more discipline, patience, compassion or boldness? These are all inside goals that, once worked on, will help you reach the outside goals faster and more effectively. It's tough to achieve more and more on the outside at the same level we are on the inside. The first man to climb Mt. Everest, Sir Edmund Hillary declared, " I had to conquer myself before I could conquer the mountain." The same is true for us. Success is an inside job. Add the necessary inside goals to your regimen today. Put a plan together for how you will develop these areas.

Strategy I will use today: _____

FEBRUARY 28

Dance with your customers. Your customers are more likely to buy from you if they like you and are comfortable with you. You get customers to like you by sounding like them, acting like them and adopting an energy level which they will be comfortable with. You repel them by going too fast when they want to go slow or by dragging when they are excited. Get in step with your customers, put them at ease and make the sale. Make a conscious effort to dance with your customers today.

Action I will take today: _____

_____

FEBRUARY
MONTH-END ACTION PLAN

_____

_____

_____

_____

_____

_____

_____

_____

_____

MARCH 1

How have you changed lately? Since last week? Since last month? Within the past year? Be very specific. Ask yourself these questions often. Be honest with your answers. Assess right now. What areas are crying out for change that you have been resisting? Adjust accordingly.

Action I will take today: _____

_____

MARCH 2

Where do you want to go? What are you going to do? What are your intentions? Don't put too much stock in the answers. Instead, look at what you're *doing*. Whatever you are doing is reality. Quit letting yourself off the hook by justifying what you are doing now by what you are going to do in the future. If what you are doing now will not take you to where you want to be in the future, then you must change your course. Which of your good intentions can you turn into action today? Be specific and then get to work!

Today I will: _____

_____

MARCH 3

Keep your cool. It's too easy to get all worked up with customers or fellow-workers when things aren't going well. Don't give up your advantage. Thomas Jefferson said, "Nothing gives a person so much advantage over another as to remain always cool and unruffled under all circumstances." If you give up your cool, you give your edge away, your commission away and probably the sale as well. Stay focused on the end result - making the sale. Don't let emotions trip you up. You can feed your ego or you can feed your family. Focus on keeping your cool at the first opportunity of "losing" it, today and every day.

Strategy I will use today: _____

_____

MARCH 4

Quit pointing the finger. Dwelling on fault and blame is a monumental energy leak. When you get all wrapped up in trying to determine who was wrong, you lose focus on how to make it right. *Focus your energy on solutions, not fault and blame.* When you are with a customer you cannot win an argument and make a sale. If you've already made the sale, you cannot win an argument and keep a customer. Make the right decision as to which it will be.

Action I will take today: _____

_____

MARCH 5

Have you bounded out of bed lately? Author Whitt Hobbs wrote, " Success is waking up in the morning, whoever you are, wherever you are, however young or old, and bounding out of bed because there is something out there that you love to do, that you believe in, that you're good at–something that's bigger than you are, and you can't wait to get at it again today." Do you feel this way about your job? If not, what would it take to get you there? Begin to address the one thing you can control to begin your bounding and intensify the passion for what you do. In sales, passion is power.

Today I will: _____

_____

MARCH 6

Send some cards. When is the last time you received a thank you card from a salesperson? Do you remember that salesperson? If you have never received one, wouldn't it stand out in your mind if you did? Take the time to say thank you. Most people spend nearly every dime they ever make and no one ever stops to say thanks. Send thank you cards. You'll stand out. You'll be remembered. You'll have others referred to you. You just could earn a customer for life. Start this practice today.

Strategy I will use today: _____

_____

MARCH 7

Do you have visions or daydreams? The difference is that visions will cost you something. When you commit to a bigger and better vision of yourself, you'll have to decide what to give up so you can blaze your vision. You'll have to trade in less productive activities like socializing at work, waiting for something to happen and watching TV for goal setting, reading, learning, practicing, prospecting and planning. If you have a *vision* that isn't going to cost you anything, it's a daydream. Daydreams don't cost much or pay much. Think of your ambitions. What are they costing you? Are they really visions or just daydreams?

Action I will take today: _____

_____

MARCH 8

When do you get ahead? Do you have to come in earlier or stay later to get ahead? Do you need to work double shifts or come in on your days off? Maybe, maybe not. There is plenty of time to get ahead during normal work hours if you have a daily plan and follow it. Henry Ford commented, "It is my observation that successful people get ahead during the time other people waste." Working long and hard is fine. Working smarter is even better. Look around at the people you work with. How do they waste time? What can you do productively during the time they are wasting?

Today I will: _____

_____

MARCH 9

Are you a promise keeper or just a promise maker? Professionals in sales under-promise and over-deliver. Maintain your integrity at all costs. You can't run far enough or fast enough to outdistance a bad reputation. It'll catch you and destroy you. Andrew Carnegie once observed, "As I grow older I pay less attention to what men say and just watch what they do." If you say it, deliver it. If you're not sure you can, err on the side of keeping your mouth closed. Resist the temptation of promising just because you think it's what your customer wants to hear. Where have you been over-promising and under-delivering? Reverse roles today.

Strategy I will use today: _____

_____

MARCH 10

Get off your "buts!" Too many times we reply to comments or questions with "yea, but" this or "yea, but" that. It's time to get off our "buts." Literally. George Washington Carver declared that, "Ninety-nine percent of failures come from people who have the habit of making excuses." Next time you're tempted to "yea, but," trade your excuse in for a solution, instead. It normally takes more creative effort to generate an excuse than it does to find a solution anyhow. Keep track of your "buts" today. Catch yourself, then focus on becoming more solution oriented.

Action I will take today: _____

_____

MARCH 11

Are you a master or a victim? When new procedures are introduced, new products, new sales techniques, etc., do you turn them into an advantage and quickly adopt to optimize opportunities? Or do you resist change, procrastinate, fight the changes and become a victim instead? It's all in how you take it. John Wooden said, "Things turn out best for those who make the best of how things turn out." Master change. Use it, advance with it, get excited about it, see the possibilities in it and use it to create a better you, a better job and better sales. After all, it's inevitable and it's going to happen with you or without you. Pinpoint an area for change which you have been resisting. Reevaluate and decide if it might be time to change from victim to master.

Today I will: _____

_____

MARCH 12

What's the true measure of your worth as a salesperson? Author/speaker Cullen Hightower said that the true measure of your worth includes all the benefits others have gained from your success. What benefits are your customers gaining from your success? Are they taken care of or are they forgotten after the sale? Do they get the right product/service for them or just whatever you want to push that day? Do they have a clear enough understanding of what they are getting and what it does and how it works? Do you want more benefits from your job? More money, more success and happiness? Then provide more benefits to your customers. You can't have one without the other.

Strategy I will use today: _____

_____

MARCH 13

When negotiating with a customer, keep the end in mind and don't get too hung up on the means for getting there. If you and the customer can keep the big picture in mind, which is, for the customer, to buy what you are selling, you'll both be on the same page and come up with creative means to make the purchase. You will foster a cooperative effort rather than an adversarial one. The sale then becomes a matter of, "Which way do you want to own it–this way or that way," and less a, "Do you want it–or take it or leave it." Make it make sense for your customer. Be solution-oriented and focused on a satisfactory end.

Action I will take today: _____

_____

MARCH 14

Logic doesn't always sell. When you are trying to persuade a customer, you can be 100% right on all points, you can logically point out in a number of areas why your product is the best on the market and why your firm stands behind what it sells better than the competition, and still not make the sale. Focus more on showing the relevance of your product to their needs, wants and desires. Remember, there are two reasons why a person will buy: they want it and/or they need it. Until they see that relevance, until they see their needs being met, it doesn't matter that your company is #1, that your product/service has the best rating or that you have the longest guarantee. Show that what you have does a better job of meeting their wants, needs and desires than the competition and you'll make the sale. There's one catch to this. In order to meet their needs you'll need to know what they are. This means you'll actually have to investigate with each customer and not just give your standard "through the motions" presentation that everyone tends to get, regardless of their situation. Ditch your pat presentations and start customizing based on what the customer in front of you is interested in. How do you find out what they're interested in? By asking questions!

Today I will: _____

_____

MARCH 15

Which road are you on? When you're trying to get somewhere, going by road is normally the fastest, most productive route. It's the same in sales, but there are different roads available. Some salespeople are looking for the *freeway.* They want to go fast and uninhibited to their destination. Others prefer an even easier path, so they have to keep a lookout for roads that are downhill since that's the only direction you can go when you're coasting. The road to long-term success in sales is not a freeway nor is it adaptable to coasting. The road to success in sales is a toll road. There's a price to pay on the road to success and it's always under construction. When pursuing your goals are you trying to take the freeway, trying to coast, or paying the price as you go? If you're on the wrong road, you don't have to stay there. What are two or three things you could start doing today to switch roads?

Strategy I will use today: _____

MARCH
MID-MONTH ACTION PLAN

_____

_____

_____

_____

_____

MARCH 16

"Knock, knock."

"Who's there?"

"It's not opportunity."

Are you still waiting for opportunity to knock on your door? Are you waiting for the door of opportunity to open for you? Stop wasting your time. Opportunity doesn't knock. It's within you right now. The question is, will you recognize it, apply it and turn it into an advantage? The door to opportunity is never closed, so stop waiting for it to open. In fact, it's been wide open all of your life and will stay wide open every day of your career. The question is, when are you going to walk through it? Stop seeing so many problems and setbacks. Start seeing them as opportunities instead. Begin to adapt a new outlook towards problems today.

Start asking yourself how you can benefit from what is happening, regardless what it is.

Action I will take today: _____

MARCH 17

Got it tough from time to time? Keep it in perspective. Booker T. Washington said, "Success is to be measured not so much by the position that one has reached in life as by the obstacles which one has overcome while trying to succeed." Remember, if you *learn* from failure, rejection and tough times, you'll take several steps forward for every one you take backward. Teddy Roosevelt remarked that there has never been a person in our history who led a life of ease, whose name was worth remembering. Keep tough times in perspective. Highlight this entry and refer to it every time things get really tough. Do it until your positive reaction to these times becomes a positive reflex.

Today I will: _____

MARCH 18

On a roll? Got a hot streak going? Keep it in perspective. Success is a double-edged sword. Nothing can create complacency like success. Nothing can isolate you, create arrogance within you, or shut your mind to new ideas and change like success can. Success is great! It's what we're all after. But to keep it you must learn how to handle it. Keep good times in perspective. Highlight this entry and refer to it every time things are going really well. Do it until a balanced response to these times becomes a positive reflex.

Strategy I will use today: _____

MARCH 19

Are you capable of selling more? Would you agree that the difference between doing what you are doing and what you are capable of doing would probably propel you to all of your financial goals? Most likely it would. We are all capable of more. We all know more than we apply. Many people know what to do, but too few wind up doing it. To increase your capabilities initially, you don't even have to learn anything new. Just make better use of what you know now. The next step is learning more and applying it as well. A small difference in capabilities can lead to a huge difference in results. What one thing could you start doing right now that would have the biggest impact on improving your capabilities? Create momentum by doing it today.

Action I will take today: _____

_____

MARCH 20

Be harder on yourself. You'll never get more out of your job or life until you start to demand more of yourself. If you always do what you've always done, you'll always get what you've always gotten. What are three primary areas in which you could start demanding more from yourself during the rest of this month? Go to work on those areas and then move onto three more. Stop accepting and settling for less than you know you can deliver. It's tough to look in the mirror on payday and know that you've stolen from yourself.

Today I will: _____

_____

MARCH 21

Quit blaming conditions. Too many salespeople blame their sales results on inventories, the competition, the weather, the market, the economy and so on. Chances are that your decisions, not conditions, have put you where you are. Too many people give credit to their decisions when things are going well and blame conditions when they are not. Get a grip! Even when conditions are unfavorable, your decisions determine how you'll respond. Will you decide that the conditions are an opportunity or an excuse to fail? Will you decide to allow the conditions to bring out the creativity that can take you to new levels, or bring out the despair that can sink you to new depths? Start making the right decisions, regardless of conditions, and you'll be going straight up while others are busy hanging their heads straight down. Watch for the next "condition" that comes along and make a conscious effort to appropriate the best decision.

Strategy I will use today: _____

_____

March 22

Interested or committed? There is a huge difference between being interested in something or actually being committed to it. Most everyone in sales is interested in getting better and becoming more successful. Being committed to becoming more successful is another matter entirely. Being committed will require action. It will require goals and a plan. Being interested is little more than raising an eyebrow. *Being committed requires raising your standards.* If you're merely *interested* in becoming more successful in sales, you'll have a lot of company. A lot of average company. Being committed is a more lonesome, focused and rewarding route.

Action I will take today: _____

_____

March 23

You can save money but you can't save time. You have to spend time. Saving time is a myth. You can't do it. You can only choose how to spend it differently. Spending time wisely is deciding how to reallocate the time you have to take advantage of high return activities and minimize or eliminate low return activities. The selling profession presents opportunities every day as to which type of activities you can choose. Think of two or three areas in which you are compromising your valuable time with low return activities. What high return activities can you replace them with?

Today I will: _____

_____

March 24

Let's revisit decisions vs. conditions today. Too many salespeople blame conditions for their problems. How convenient. Most of the problems and frustrations we face every day are brought upon by decisions we have made in the past. In fact, a valid argument would be that wherever you are in your career today, good or bad, is a result of decisions you have made. Want better results? Make better decisions. *Decide* to learn more about selling and your product. *Decide* to develop your attitude on a daily basis. *Decide* to plan, prospect and prepare. *Decide* to do the most productive thing every minute of every day. *Decide* to follow-up with your customers. *Decide* to set goals. *Decide* to demand more from yourself. What decisions have you made in the past that are causing you current pain?

What can you do to learn from them? Remember, your career rises and falls on the daily decisions you make. Right decisions made repeatedly everyday compound success. If you don't do anything to improve the decisions you are making, then you are still making a decision—*a decision to stay with the average crowd and to fail.*

Strategy I will use today: _____

_____

MARCH 25

A decision isn't a rest stop. In fact, never settle for making a decision until you've taken the first step of action towards its implementation. Decisions without action are merely good intentions. You kill the potential momentum and results a decision can bring by stopping to rest. It's often too hard to start back up. Think of some good decisions you've made lately that have been rendered impotent by inaction. What can you do to revive and profit from them today?

Action I will take today: _____

_____

MARCH 26

Do you believe in your product/service? Do you believe in your company? Do you believe in yourself? Speaker/writer Herb True observed that many people can become successful when other people do not believe in them, but very few can succeed when they don't believe in themselves. It's true. In fact, when it comes to believing in themselves, some salespeople are agnostic. Even if you do believe in yourself, do you believe strongly enough? Can you see yourself taking quantum leaps in your future or just limping along? Whatever your level of self-belief, what can you do to make it better? Would higher self-esteem help? Think of three actions that would help create more self-esteem. Self-esteem will breed confidence and confidence will build your self-belief. Go to work on your three actions today.

Today I will: _____

_____

MARCH 27

Even if you're not preparing, you're preparing for *something*. When you were in school did you prepare for tests? For speeches? For entrance exams? If you did prepare, you felt more confident didn't you? Less stressful? More in control? It's the same in sales, only sales pays a lot better than school ever did. What you may not realize is that even if you're not preparing, you are. If you're not consciously preparing for success you *are* unconsciously preparing to fail. Either way, you are preparing for something. Has your preparation been to consciously succeed or has it defaulted to preparing for failure? This is another one of those decisions (not conditions) that can either move you up above the crowd in sales or keep you anchored to mediocrity. Evaluate your preparation ethic and determine which result you are spending your time preparing for: more sales success or mediocrity.

Strategy I will use today: _____

_____

MARCH 28

Some salespeople feel that they are often misunderstood by their prospects and customers. That's usually because they are putting the cart before the horse. It's important to remember that it's your job to first try to understand the customer and then to be understood. You are supposed to spend your time first listening and then explaining, not trying to jump in and explain before you fully understand your customer and what is going on. In their excitement, too many salespeople jump in and try to finish a customer's sentence and thoughts for them. Can you remember doing this? It normally happens so fast and so often, we do it without even realizing it. We jump to conclusions, hearing what we want to hear and not taking a breath and listening for what's important; what the customer is really saying. Become more aware of your listening habits. Spend more time trying to understand, then worry about being understood. Your customers are more willing to listen to your solutions *after* they are certain you understand their situation. When you begin focusing on this discipline, your customers will notice and so will you–on payday.

Action I will take today: _____

MARCH 29

Cut yourself some slack. If you don't have it all together yet, if you're still struggling with changes and the new disciplines needed to get to the next level in your career, it's okay. As a famous speaker once said, "Touchdowns in football and life don't usually happen in 70 yard increments. It's more like three yards and a cloud of dust." None of us is born with the mindset of a champion or the skills of a sales superstar. *These have to be developed one day at a time.* One skill at a time. One mistake at a time. Remember, champions don't become champions in the ring. They are merely recognized in the ring. The 'becoming' happens during their daily routine. Take the little victories as they come. Which little improvements or victories have come and gone in the past few days that you've taken for granted? Think about them, be grateful for them and realize that as small as they may seem, they are part of the grand journey to the next level above the crowd.

Today I will: _____

_____

MARCH 30

If you could change something about your job, what would it be? What would have the greatest impact on your performance? The management? The advertising? The product? The pricing? The competition? Your co-workers? Your compensation plan? Company benefits? What would it be? Author Leo Tolstoy said, "Everyone thinks of changing the world, no one thinks of changing himself." Focus your efforts today on the things you can control. It's the one exercise that provides the greatest return on energy.

Strategy I will use today: _____

_____

MARCH 31

How many different objections do you hear in a given week? Write them down. How many are there? Hundreds? Dozens? More than likely, it's less than a dozen isn't it? Are they pretty much the same ones you heard last week, last month and last year? Do you let the thought of objections psych you out, even though there are very few you always have to deal with and they're the same ones again and again? Objections like, "I'll have to think it over," "I'll need to shop your price," or "I have to consult with another before I can decide" keep coming up. Doesn't it make sense to learn how to handle them once and for all? Most of the objections were here last year and they're going to be here next year. They're not going to go away. Take your list of objections and put together your best scripts for handling them. Focus on one objection for two weeks or for an entire month if you want. Master it. Learn several methods to reflexively overcome it. In a matter of weeks or months you will have mastered every objection you ever hear. Most salespeople go through an entire career and never get this done. Take a systematic approach and build the skills and confidence to handle objections. They're not going anywhere. And if you know the plays the other team is going to run in advance, shouldn't you win a few more games? Which objection will you start mastering today?

Action I will take today: _____

MARCH
MONTH-END ACTION PLAN

_____

_____

_____

_____

_____

_____

_____

_____

_____

_____

_____

_____

APRIL 1

Want an edge? Read a book. Books make you think. They broaden your mind. They add perspective to life. Most people don't go to the trouble of reading books. There are hundreds of sales and motivational books available. The American Bookseller's Association estimates that 58% of the population has not completed a book since high school and 70% haven't visited a book store in the past five years. It's easy to read consistently if you have a plan. Buy a book and take the total number of pages and divide that number by the days in the month. Read that number of pages each day and you'll read one book per month. (If the book has 240 pages and the month has 30 days, you'd only have to read 8 pages per day!) Some people read four and five books per month using this simple method. Like anything else in life, reading is easier if you'll plan it and turn it into a daily goal. Start your reading this week.

Action I will take today: _____

_____

APRIL 2

Are you flexible? The American Management Association predicts that flexibility will be the number one quality needed to succeed in the 21st Century. That's because our markets, customers and products will continue to change at rapid pace. Will you be able to keep up? Flexibility is a mindset. Unsuccessful people have made the habit of recirculating old ideas. They become entrapped in rigidity. The more you learn and improve yourself, the more flexible you will become. *The key is to become flexible without losing focus* In which areas could you stand to replace some rigidity with flexibility? Open your mind, improve your skills and go to work on them today

Today I will: _____

_____

APRIL 3

What's your competitive advantage? What makes you different? Is it your knowledge, your attitude, your work ethic? Your networking skills? Do you have the competitive advantages that you'd like, or are you too close to the rest of the pack? Take an inventory on yourself to determine what your strengths are and work on enhancing the top two or three. Create your own area of uniqueness and use it to increase your viability, marketability and competitive edge.

The more you distance yourself from the pack, the quicker you'll be selling above the crowd.

Strategy I will use today: _____

_____

April 4

What are the critical success factors in your job? The Harvard Business Journal wrote that each job typically has five to seven critical points to address for optimum achievement. In sales they are normally building rapport with the customer, investigating for needs, presenting the product, overcoming objections, closing the sale, getting appointments and networking. Come up with the critical success factors for your job. Rate yourself on a scale of 1 to 10 in each area. Determine the positive points that make up your score in each area and reinforce them. Then put a plan together to work toward a higher level in each critical area. This incremental improvement plan will keep you focused and continually moving in the right direction. Remember, the lowest score in any area is the highest point you can reach overall as a professional in sales. Find your factors, rate yourself and put a plan together to get to a 10 in each area. Review yourself and reset the critical success factors quarterly.

Action I will take today: _____

_____

April 5

Seek and you shall sell. Are you continually seeking out new information about your product/service selling skills, market and competition in order to position yourself to sell more? Too many salespeople fall into the trap of underachievers when they stop seeking new information. What have you sought out lately (sought out, not had put in front of you)? Don't just sit back and wait for information to fall into your lap. The whole pack will have that same information. Enhance your competitive advantage, self-confidence and self-esteem by committing to an ongoing quest of seeking out and then applying new information in your field. Work today with the mindset of a seeker.

Today I will: _____

_____

APRIL 6

Ever feel like you're in a rut? Every salesperson can feel this way from time to time. The good news is that you have the key to climb out of it. Harvard philosopher William James wrote, "The greatest discovery in our time is that human beings can alter their lives by altering their minds." You don't have to wait for something to *happen*. You can act upon yourself and snap out of whatever rut you're in. The best cure for a sluggish mind or a mind in a rut is to *disturb its routine*. What are three or four things you've read in this book so far that are part of your action plan, that you can focus on to disturb your own routine the next time a rut starts to set in? Be prepared and you won't be in the next rut for long.

Strategy I will use today: _____

_____

APRIL 7

Do you get confused? When you do, chances are that you lose some of your "punch" in performing your job. Vince Lombardi said that it's hard to be aggressive when you are confused. Preparation reduces confusion. If there are areas you get lost in, go back and build your confidence in those areas. Confusion weakens you. It takes the power out of your personality and your presentation. Think of an area you keep having trouble with; a certain product's features, a recurring objection from a customer, a comparison with a competitive product, etc., and solidify this area by letting repetition and preparation take the place of confusion.

Action I will take today: _____

_____

APRIL 8

"That's good!" Author/insurance executive, W. Clement Stone, made this short phrase famous by expressing it whenever anything happened, good or bad. If what happened didn't seem good, he said it anyway and that changed his thinking into looking for and finding the good in whatever transpired. Stone also had a philosophy on "reverse paranoia." He felt that anything that happened or was done in his life was part of a worldwide conspiracy to make him more successful. Adopt the powerful outlook of "that's good," and reverse paranoia to turn everything that happens to you into something productive and profitable. It's a great substitute for a pity party.

Today I will: _____

_____

APRIL 9

What's your vision for your career and your future? Does it energize you? Do you have a vision at all? Revisit the vision you have for your future in sales. Create it or recreate it so that it generates energy, motivation and inspiration. A vision will add meaning to each customer and each day. It'll prevent you from simply going through the motions. Think about your vision. Write it down with your goals. Look at it daily. To judge its power and effectiveness, you must ask yourself what it is causing you to do. Is it what you want? Is it enough?

Strategy I will use today: _____

_____

APRIL 10

Want to motivate yourself? Start finishing things. Finishing is motivating. Most people are great at getting started and poor at finishing. Harvard philosopher, William James wrote, "Nothing in the world is more fatiguing as having an unfinished task." What unfinished tasks do you have lying around? If they're worth finishing, get them done. If not, get rid of the excess baggage and go on to something you can commit to completing. Wipe your slate clean before you begin another project. Large or small, have a plan for finishing it. Finishing is a habit. A very motivational one.

Action I will take today: _____

_____

APRIL 11

Having trouble getting rid of bad habits? That's probably because you're trying to get _rid_ of them without having something to _replace_ them with. Think of the two or three worst habits you have: procrastination, call reluctance, not planning your day, wasting too much time at work, etc. Determine what you will do to replace that habit with something productive. Turn it into a plan and be specific. Trying to break bad habits is a waste of time without a sound plan for replacing them with good habits.

Today I will: _____

_____

APRIL 12

Potential and *ability* are two of the most overrated factors in sales today. Don't rely on them to get you very far without the added ingredient of effort. The sales ranks are filled with unfulfilled potential and unapplied abilities. Success is the result of an accumulation of effort. Successful people take potential and ability and apply them. They turn them into action. Think of a couple of areas where you have greater abilities and potential than your results have been showing. Isn't it time to add some extra effort and action to that potential?

Strategy I will use today: _____

_____

APRIL 13

Stop for a moment and review your goals. How do they look? Are they impressive? Are they big enough? How will you feel when you achieve them? Now for the really important question: What are they causing you to do on a daily basis that is different from what you'd be doing if you had no goals? What goals are is not nearly as important as what they make you do. If they look impressive on paper but are creating no action or no changes, if they haven't elevated your thinking or performance, take action or toss them out and start over. Goals were never intended to result in window dressing. They are designed to result in action.

Action I will take today: _____

_____

APRIL 14

Are you forgetting something at home? Too many salespeople rush out to conquer the sales world and soon forget where they came from. Take care of your home front before you try to conquer the world. Putting family first takes integrity and well-grounded priorities. If family is set on the backburner, it will eventually scorch. If you want your success journey to be long lasting and more rewarding than you ever thought possible, you'll need to remember to bring your family along for the ride. What can you do to add more balance to your family or relationship life?

Today I will: _____

_____

April 15

Clarify. How many times do you jump in to handle an objection only to find out what you thought was the problem wasn't the real problem at all? Clarify objections by restating them to the customer. Clear them up before you try to overcome them. When a customer says that your product/service is "too expensive," are they really worried about the price of the item or about the monthly payment? Chances are, you can get creative and fit it in a budget without every having to cut your price or switch them to a less expensive model. When you hear an objection, stop, breathe, and clarify before rushing in and making a mess of things.

Strategy I will use today: _____

_____

April
Mid-Month Action Plan

_____

_____

_____

_____

_____

_____

_____

_____

April 16

Put a premium on persistence. The founders of McDonald's adopted a creed that said: "Press on. Nothing in the world can take the place of persistence. Talent will not. The world is full of unsuccessful men with talent. Genius will not. The world is full of educated derelicts. Persistence and determination alone are omnipotent." Talent and genius go right up there in the "potential" category when not combined with effort and action. Keep this in perspective. How many really bright or talented people do you know who don't maximize their abilities? Don't fall into the same trap.

Action I will take today: _____

_____

APRIL 17

Elevate or devastate. It's your choice. If you're not doing something to consciously elevate your attitude, disposition and outlook each day, you are devastating it by default. It may not show up in a day or a week. But soon your mind, habits and enthusiasm will be so far off track you'll spend most of your time just trying to get back to where you were; much less moving forward. It's easier to stay on track than to get back on track. How is your daily dose of attitude and motivation coming? Is it elevating or devastating? Stay on track and you never have to worry about getting back on the track.

Today I will: _____

_____

APRIL 18

Find "it." You'll never be able to handle "I'll think it over" until you find out what the "it" is. Too many salespeople dismiss customers without even attempting to find the "it." Is "it" the price, the payment, the color, the features, the need to discuss it with another, the need to shop around, etc? You can't go any further until you find "it." Remember, clarify, clarify, clarify! Once you find "it," you can assess and address "it." The best way to find "it" is to ask, "Mr. Customer, I understand your wanting to think it over, but there must be some reason you're hesitating. Do you mind if I ask what 'it' is?" If they don't tell you what "it" is then make it easier for them by offering choices: "If there was one thing holding you back from wrapping this up today, is it the styling, the features, the color, something about our company or is it the price?" Always put what you really think "it" is as the last choice. (Hint: "It's" usually the price.)

Strategy I will use today: _____

_____

Selling Above The Crowd

APRIL 19

No more New Year's resolutions. There are two groups of people in sales, those who talk and those who take–action. Too many salespeople have the New Year's resolution syndrome: "I'll go on a diet after the first of the year," and then they shovel down another double-meat cheeseburger, fries and shake because it's only November. Salespeople's resolutions sound like this, "I'll start my follow-up program after summer starts," or "I'll start organizing my daily schedule and setting goals after I'm back from vacation," and it goes on and on and never gets done. Determine whether you are going to be part of the group that studies the race or joins the race. Walk away from the group who would rather discuss than decide anything. Take action and leave the "pack in the back."

Action I will take today: _____

APRIL 20

Replace "have" with "make." Don't just *have* a nice day. What will you do to *make* it one? Don't rely on having a good month. Put a specific plan of action together to make it one. And don't hold your breath hoping to have a great career. You'll need to make it happen as well. "Having" relies too much on good intentions and wishful thinking. "Making" takes control and directs it with action. Take greater charge of your destiny. Change your thinking and your vocabulary.

Today I will: _____

APRIL 21

What's holding you back? Look at your goals. Where do you want to be? Shift your thinking to a higher level and ask yourself what is holding you back from being there right *now*. Take action on those items. It's estimated that 80% of what keeps us from being where we want to be comes from internal sources. Only 20% is affected by what happens on the outside. Successful people look at themselves first. These are the areas they can control. Take the top couple of things holding you back and write down 10 to 20 ideas on how to address each area. Then go on to the next couple of items and keep taking action. To get to the next level takes focus and a plan. Work on these "holdback" areas daily.

Strategy I will use today: _____

APRIL 22

Procrastination kills momentum. Procrastination kills creativity. Procrastination kills potential. Procrastination kills progress and it will kill your career as well. Procrastination is a habit. As with all habits, you can't just break it. You have to replace it with something else; <u>action</u>. Start each day by doing the most productive tasks first, regardless of whether they are pleasurable or you dislike them. By doing this, even if you are procrastinating certain projects, they won't be those which bring you the greatest return. Taking action is like flexing a muscle. The more you get used to flexing and using it, the stronger it is and the easier it is to use.

Action I will take today: _____

_____

APRIL 23

Quit playing "some day." "Some day I'll do this." "Some day I'll have that." Eliminate "some day" from your vocabulary. Some day can be an excuse to procrastinate. It can be a reason to become comfortable with today's mediocrity. Before long, "some day" turns into "one of these days" and what you'll find is that "one of these days" usually winds up being "never." Remember that there is no reason why today cannot be one of the most productive, impacting days of your career. Live and work in "today."

Today I will: _____

_____

APRIL 24

Too many people waste their time waiting for the sales profession to "show them the money." This business shows you the money when you show the business the skills. How is your skill development coming? Are you focusing more on what you are *becoming* than on what you *get?* Specifically, how have you *become* more lately? The good news is that as you become more you will get more. Show the business the skills and it will show you and throw you the money.

Strategy I will use today: _____

_____

April 25

You can't fake it. Are you prepared for today? Are you prepared for your next customer? Joe Frazier once said, "You can map out a fight plan or a life plan but when the action starts, you're down to your reflexes. That's where your practice shows. If you cheated on the practice in the dark of the morning, you'll get found out under the bright lights." When you are with your customers, the bright lights are shining. Have you prepared yourself for them? Have you studied and practiced? What can you do right now to get ready for when the lights come on?

Action I will take today: _____

_____

April 26

Stop digging. When you're in a rut, have you ever noticed how things seem to go from bad to worse? It seems, sometimes, that the harder you press, the tougher it gets. The key to getting out of a rut is to *stop digging* - if you don't, it'll turn into a grave. Instead of pressing, release. Step back, regroup, evaluate and change course if necessary. In our stubbornness, it's easy to keep pressing and pushing, even though it may be along the wrong path. The next time you're in a rut, stop digging, redirect, and start climbing.

Today I will: _____

_____

April 27

Is your aim boring or soaring? United Technologies Corporation has a creed that reads, "The greatest waste of our natural resources is the number of people who never achieve their potential. Get out of that slow lane. Shift into the fast lane. If you think you can't, you won't. If you think you can, there's a good chance you will. Just making the effort will make you feel like a new person. Reputations are made by searching for things that can't be done and doing them. Aim low - boring. Aim high - *SOARING*." Enough said.

Strategy I will use today: _____

_____

APRIL 28

There are four words to remember for success in sales: **Add value to customers.** You add value when you care enough to find out their needs, take the time to match their needs with the right features and follow through enough to take care of them long after you've cashed the commission check. There are four words to remember for failure in sales: *Take advantage of customers.* You take advantage of customers when you breech their trust in you by caring more about the short-term effects of the sale than the long-term benefits of a mutually productive relationship. Which four words are moving your motives?

Action I will take today: _____

_____

APRIL 29

Reduce it to the ridiculous. Part of your job is to make it make sense for your customers. They want to buy your product/service, they're just looking for justification; they want to feel good about it. If you are $1,000 away from what your customer wants to spend, reduce it to the ridiculous. On a five year loan (with interest), $1,000 is just $20 per month. Twenty dollars per month is just 70 cents per day; the equivalent of about a coke per day. Would you rather try and negotiate over $1,000 or over a coke per day? What's easier to find in your customer's budget? Maybe they can see $1,000 standing between them and what they want, but they can't see a soft drink preventing the pleasure of getting what they want. Make it make sense. Reducing it to the ridiculous makes your customers feel better about spending more than they planned. It justifies it.

Today I will: _____

_____

APRIL 30

Where's your focus? Is it on the process or the product? Sometimes we focus so much on the outcome - the product - we get off track with following the process that will take us to the sale. When we take our eyes off the process or get away from the basics, the desired outcome can become very elusive. Slow down, stay on track, find constant ways to improve your process and the product will be right around the corner. First things first. What are two ways you can improve the most vital parts of your sales process?

Strategy I will use today: _____

_____

APRIL
MONTH-END ACTION PLAN

_____

_____

_____

_____

_____

_____

_____

_____

_____

_____

_____

MAY 1

Use your emotions to improve your sales. When you feel disappointed, it typically means you have an expectation that you did not meet. Ask yourself why you didn't meet it. What can you learn from the disappointment? Regroup and then go after it again. Remember, if you first don't succeed, find out *why,* then try again. Use disappointment as a catalyst and inspiration to learn and do better next time.

Action I will take today: _____

_____

MAY 2

Use the emotion of feeling inadequate to discover where you are falling short. This will help you recognize your strengths and weaknesses. If you don't feel up to speed in a particular part of the sales process, identify it, then go to work to improve it. By continually evaluating all of the steps in the process and singling out the ones to focus on improving, you raise your overall performance in every area.

Today I will: _____

_____

MAY 3

Use the emotion of being afraid as an impetus for more preparation. Is there a certain kind of customer you fear? How about a particular objection to buying? Use fear as feedback to correct your course and you can turn fear into power. Preparation reduces stress and builds confidence. Confidence combined with developing a plan for these weak areas eliminates fear. Chances are that the types of objections or customers you fear will always be there. The good news is that customers and objections you fear are feared by the salespeople you compete against. They're not going away. You might as well prepare yourself to handle them better and turn them to your advantage.

Strategy I will use today: _____

_____

MAY 4

Feeling the emotion of frustration is a good thing. When you feel frustrated it means that you are expecting and demanding more from yourself and are not willing to settle for the status quo. Frustration will help keep you out of comfort zones by disturbing your inner self until you are forced to change your situation. Use frustration as the inner fire to push yourself to new levels.

Action I will take today: _____

_____

MAY 5

Avoid the emotion of anger at all costs. It clouds everything else you do. When you get angry with a customer, remember that you seldom win an argument and still make the sale. You can be 100% right and have all the facts on your side, but the customer ultimately saddles you with a loss by leaving without buying your product or service. Disarm a customer's anger by focusing on solutions and not the problem. Don't waste energy dwelling on who was right or wrong. There's not much money in it.

Today I will: _____

_____

MAY 6

When you feel guilty about your performance or behavior, it's your way of telling yourself that you've violated the rules, cut short the process, softened your work ethic, etc. Use guilt as an opportunity to affirm that the violation will not occur again. Hold yourself accountable to higher standards of discipline and then go on. Don't dwell or beat yourself up over what happened. You are in this for the long haul and will progress faster and more effectively if you realize you'll fall short from time to time. Commit to learning and correcting the situation and then moving on, stronger than before.

Strategy I will use today: _____

_____

MAY 7

When you legitimately feel overloaded or overwhelmed it may mean you are trying to do too much at once. This makes you feel out of control. Refocus! Assess the most important things you want to accomplish and write them down. Then prioritize them. Put the less important leftovers on the back burner for now. Take the top item on your list and come up with several ideas and steps for getting it done. This will create momentum and give you back the sense of control you need to succeed. Once you have accomplished the first task, move on to the next one. "Shoot" at your objectives with a rifle and a scope, not with a 12-gauge shotgun.

Action I will take today: _____

_____

MAY 8

Be patient with your growth process. If you have put realistic goals together with solid plans and are following them and focusing on continual learning and self-improvement, cut yourself some slack. Remember that you are developing skills and growing a career; you're not growing a weed. It won't happen overnight. You wouldn't expect to plant a seed in your yard and then go out the next day and find a tree. Nor will you hit all your goals as quickly as you'd like. Focus on the process. Enjoy the process. Massage the process. Master the process and the results will be there. Trying to shortcut the process shifts you from growing to wandering in circles.

Today I will: _____

_____

MAY 9

When do you feel better about paying for something, before or after you see the value in the product? When are you willing to pay more, before or after you see the value? Your customers are the same way. If you are trying to sell price before value, they'll never have a chance to perceive enough value to justify the price. Rarely does anyone feel great about spending money until they've had a chance to see exactly what they're getting for their money. Make sure your customers get that chance.

Strategy I will use today: _____

_____

MAY 10

Do you like to hear objections to buying your product? You should. A good, strong objection is a solid buying sign. The key is in learning how to handle the objections, not fearing them and hoping they don't come up. They will. A real objection is all that is standing in the way of making the sale. It's the customer's way of telling you what you have to do to sell them the product.

Use an objection as a stepping stone to closing the sale, not a stumbling block.

Action I will take today: _____

_____

MAY 11

Isolate and close. When you hear an objection from a customer, isolate it to determine that what you are hearing is the only objection. The two key words to isolating are "other than." For instance, "other than fitting the payments in your budget, is there anything else holding you back from wrapping this up right now?" You need to know what you have to work with and what you are up against. Isolating lets you know. If you're tired of overcoming one objection just to have your customer come up with another one, learn to isolate each and every objection you hear. It's your way of getting a commitment from the customer. You should ask so that you know exactly what is standing in the way of closing the deal.

Today I will: _____

_____

MAY 12

Learn to clarify objections. When you hear an objection, it's vital to make sure you understand exactly what it is before rushing in and trying to handle it. When a customer wants to "think it over," clarify what they want to think over. Is it the features, the color, the financing, the price? If a customer says, "You guys sure want a lot of money for this thing," reply as follows, "When you say we want a lot of money for this, are you concerned about the total price, will you be writing a check, or are you concerned with what the payments will be if you finance it?" If the customer is financing the purchase, the price may not matter at all. It may just be a matter of making the payments affordable, which can possibly be done without ever touching the price. Clarify means to clear up. Clear up your next objection before you rush in and wind up chasing the wrong one.

Strategy I will use today: _____

_____

MAY 13

Don't be your own worst enemy. We create most of our own objections by skipping a sales step somewhere along the line. If we fail to build rapport with a customer, don't investigate properly for wants and needs, rush through a presentation or try to go right for the close before they see the value, for example, we are creating objections for ourselves. One of the best ways to overcome objections is before they come up by avoiding shortcuts during the road to the sale, treating the customer like a serious buyer, and building the value of the product. The customer will come up with enough objections on their own; you don't need to create additional ones by taking shortcuts.

Action I will take today: _____

_____

MAY 14

How long have you been "riding your horse?" Some of us have been doing the same things, working the same routine, saying the same phrases, thinking the same thoughts for so long that the horse we're riding is wearing out and slowing down. When the horse you've been riding dies, dismount! Nothing in your business stays the same and neither can you. Take your "horse's" pulse today.

Today I will: _____

_____

MAY 15

Too many of us blame poor days, weeks, and months on conditions such as the weather, the market and the economy. This is the easy way out. The fact is that most of the time we are to blame for failing to plan for these things. We know they're out there and might arise. Plan. Be proactive. Put things in motion to "bullet-proof" your future. Remember, the future is that time when you'll wish you had done something differently than you are doing now.

Strategy I will use today: _____

MAY
MID-MONTH ACTION PLAN

_____

_____

_____

_____

_____

_____

_____

MAY 16

Do you take time to evaluate each day and make adjustments to make the next day better? It is important to live our careers looking forward, but remember to learn from it by looking back. Don't dwell–just a quick glance and go forward. Replay today's "game film" in your head before you plan tomorrow. Notice what went right and wrong. Make adjustments accordingly for improved results. Do this daily. It's the key to never-ending improvement.

Action I will take today: _____

_____

MAY 17

What has your attitude been when problems and challenges arise? Your problems aren't the problem, it's what you let them do to you that's the problem. Remember the story of David and Goliath? Everyone looked at Goliath and thought he was too big to kill. David looked at him and thought he was too big to miss! Change your outlook, and your problems become victories. Focus constantly on improving your attitude toward problems. There will always be problems. Develop the mentality to handle them properly before they ever arise.

Today I will: _____

_____

MAY 18

One of the major differences between people are the questions they ask. Some people wonder, "How can this happen to me?" while others ask, "What can I learn from this?" Most people ask, "Why me?" while others ponder, "How can I use this?" Some people wonder how they can get more while others plan on how they can *become* more. Some want to know what's in it for them while others seek to find how they can add value to others. Can you see the pattern and the differences in questions? Can you see how the questions you ask yourself can move you to higher levels? Which set of questions have you been asking lately? Change the questions you ask and you can change your life.

Strategy I will use today: _____

_____

MAY 19

Are you getting the most out of each day? Remember that today isn't a "practice session" for something better tomorrow. We don't get a single moment back, much less a whole day. Get the most out of today. Plan it, execute it and make something happen. The time you have today is just like a taxi meter; it's going to keep ticking and ticking whether you are moving or standing still. Keep moving.

Action I will take today: _____

_____

MAY 20

The more you sweat in training, the less you'll bleed in battle. Too many salespeople are not only bleeding in the "battle" to sell their customers, they're hemorrhaging. Refine your skills in private and you'll have more victories in public. There are no shortcuts. Training is not glamorous or overly exciting. It doesn't work overnight. But it does work. Choose the "pain" of daily training and skill development or the "pain" of losing more deals. Pick one or the other. There is no third choice.

Today I will: _____

_____

MAY 21

Do you know how to handle "no" or "maybe" when you hear it from a customer? If your answer is "no" or "maybe," you've got some work to do. Especially since these responses from customers are not going to disappear. When a customer says "no," he normally means, "not yet–tell me more and ask me again later." "No" doesn't mean forever. Use it as a stepping stone to close the sale.

Strategy I will use today: _____

_____

MAY 22

Selling is the art of managing perceptions. You must manage your customer's perception that what you are selling is worth the price and that they need it now. You must also manage the perception that if they don't buy your product and decide to buy someone else's, they are making a mistake. The key to doing this is to build value in the product/service and excitement and urgency to own it. This is technique, not pressure. The more you can get your customer involved in the selling process, the more urgent and excited they'll become. Indifferent presentations of the product produce indifferent reactions from the buyer. Become more enthusiastic. Ask more questions of the buyer to uncover hot buttons. Build value and urgency and you'll build sales.

Action I will take today: _____

_____

MAY 23

Are you an expert in your field? Customers look for sincerity and credibility before they lay out their money. Do you *really* know your product/service? If you're faking it, you'll get found out time and time again. Instill confidence and you are building value in your product and yourself. Customers are willing to let a professional take control of the process, but they resent wasting time dealing or negotiating with an amateur.

Today I will: _____

_____

MAY 24

Can you prove it? Customers may doubt what you say but they'll believe what they read. Evidence defeats belief. Establish an "evidence manual" with specific data on your product/service. It could include write ups from consumer magazines, comparisons with competitor's products, referral letters, quality or service awards won, citations of your business and company for community involvement, awards that you have won and other public recognition for you and your company. An evidence manual proves your case and shows why the customer should buy from you. Talk is cheap. Seeing it in print strikes deep.

Strategy I will use today: _____

_____

MAY 25

Do you look the part? Too many "professionals" in sales try to pull off, "Look at me, I'm a pro" with wrinkled, out of style clothing, unpolished shoes, shabbily kept hair and poor manners and grammar. Bad breath is an incredible sales killer. The good news is that all of these things can be fixed and refined. Looking the part is a vital ingredient in managing perceptions and in gaining an edge over the competition. Take a good look in the mirror. Would you buy something from who you see?

Action I will take today: _____

_____

MAY 26

People judge the message by the messenger. In addition to appearance, how is the rest of your presentation? Pleasing personality? Good eye contact? Confident? Too many salespeople act like they just lost a coin toss and "had" to go out and wait on a customer. They mumble, look defeated, shuffle around and just go through the motions to pick up another paycheck. What message are you sending? You can fake it but you can't fool most people for long. Work on improving your message and your delivery. Even if it's good now, what can you do to make it better?

Today I will: _____

_____

MAY 27

Have a "can do" attitude. Too many salespeople spend more energy finding reasons why something cannot be done than they do finding reasons why it can. Don't get so locked into procedure that you turn your customers off with a seemingly uncooperative and uncaring attitude. Stay positive! Even if it's something that you can't do, offer alternative solutions. Avoid saying no.

Strategy I will use today: _____

_____

MAY 28

Lose your "hard sell" hyped-up message and delivery. It can make you sound desperate and cast doubt on your integrity. Professionals can build just as much urgency and excitement by keeping an even tone with a matter-of-fact delivery. Use reasonable tone and inflection to emphasize your key points and learn to plant seeds of urgency as you go through your presentation. Being enthusiastic does not mean you have to be loud.

Action I will take today: _____

_____

MAY 29

Planting seeds of urgency can be as easy as using phrases like, "I think we have a few of those left–they've been selling like hotcakes," or, "It looks like we've only got three of those left–they've been very popular," or, "Yes, we do carry those and they're an excellent choice–in fact they're one of our best sellers!" You get the idea. Dropping these little seeds of urgency into the conversation helps set the tone for your presentation. You'll need to come up with your own seeds based on what you sell. What are three phrases you can use to build urgency in getting your product? Write them down and practice incorporating them into your presentation.

Today I will: _____

_____

MAY 30

Don't get frustrated when you don't have exactly what your prospect is looking for. Frustration is contagious and can be passed on to your prospect. Feel good and focus on what you do have. You'll be amazed at how flexible most people are when it comes to colors, equipment, features and the like. If they want a white product and you don't have white, point to what you do have and say, "I don't see a white one. Out of blue, silver and red, which do you prefer?" Act like there *ought* to be another choice. Stay on track, ask lots of questions and make what you have fit their needs. Take the approach that your customer is one who will be flexible rather than automatically resigning yourself to the defeatist conclusion that he won't.

Strategy I will use today: _____

_____

May 31

When you can't get a buyer to do something right away, be patient. Buyers are doing more research than ever before. Getting impatient or pushy will sabotage your efforts. Make it your place to ensure that they are making the best choice and help them through the process. Remember that two of your jobs are to make the purchase make sense and to stop them from making a mistake; and remember that if they don't buy or buy from anyone else they *are* making a mistake. Stay with them with gentle persistence and value-building logic to help get them to the right choice.

Action I will take today: _____

May
Month-End Action Plan

_____

_____

_____

_____

_____

_____

_____

_____

_____

JUNE 1

Remember to use objections to your advantage. They are buying signs. In fact, when you hear an objection, your customer is actually giving you something to work with in trying to close the sale. The worst situation is a customer who doesn't buy and gives no reason–in this case you have nothing to work with. An objection is your clue and cue to what it will take to close the deal. Pay attention, isolate it and then go to work to close on it. Stop dreading objections and running from them. Stop dreaming of the day when you will sell the best product/service at the best price, with no competition, to hordes of people who just can't get enough of it. That day will never come. Uncover objections and turn them into sales.

Action I will take today: _____

_____

JUNE 2

Sometimes it's tough for a customer to come right out and say "yes" to your product even if they want and need it. Learn to read between the lines and look for signs that they really want to do business. Signs such as when they start asking more detailed questions, try to get last minute concessions, or try one last negotiation technique are indications that a good either/or assumptive closing question may be in order. When you feel you're at this point, make it easy for your prospect by saying something like, "Well, John, looks like we found the perfect car for you and your family. Did you want the paperwork in your name or both names?" Don't ask if they want it. Instead assume they want it and ask how they want to own it.

Today I will: _____

_____

JUNE 3

All of the best closing questions do not allow for the answer "no." Never ask if they "want it" or if you can wrap it up for them. They can say no. Instead, maintain control of the closing opportunity by asking an either/or closing question which assumes that they want it–it just seeks to find out how they want to own it, for instance, "Did you want the 36 or 48 month option, the green or the blue one, or $1,000 down or $2,000 down?" If you have done a good job of building value in yourself, your company and the product, ask a closing question that sounds like you expect them to make the purchase. You've earned the right.

Strategy I will use today: _____

JUNE 4

When you ask a good either/or closing question, nothing bad will happen. You will either close the sale or flush out an objection. Either way, you are making progress. Obviously, if the closing question results in the customer choosing one of the options you offer, you have been successful. The other side is that if you succeed in flushing out an objection, you have gotten one step closer to making the sale. Asking more closing questions leads to more sales. Just make sure you are asking the right type of closing question–an either/or, not a yes or no. Write down and practice three of these today.

Action I will take today: _____

JUNE 5

To make a closing question even more effective, make a positive statement before asking the either/or closing question. "It looks like we found the perfect car, Bob. Did you want to register the title in your name or both names?" "You're going to love your new pendant, Jenny, did you want the 18" or 24" chain?" "This stereo is going to do everything you told me you were looking for, John. Can we deliver it this afternoon or would in the morning be better?" Saying something positive before asking a closing question is called an assumptive close. Once again, focus on the premise that they will make the purchase, the only question being how they want to own it. Practice three assumptive closes customized to your product/service until they sound natural and flow easily.

Today I will: _____

JUNE 6

Your closes can be rendered useless. You can learn and memorize dozens of closes. You can know them frontward and backward. You can also forget about them ever working if you don't take care of the first part of the sales process: building rapport, investigating for needs, giving meaningful presentations and demonstrations. Closes will not bail you out of a bad first impression, lack of product knowledge or not matching their wants and needs with your product/service. If you skip steps during the first part of the sales process, the only closing tool you will have is price. You'll have to hope you can make it cheap enough so that they'll take it anyway.

Strategy I will use today: _____

_____

JUNE 7

Are you *good* at what you're doing? If you are, it can be a mixed blessing. Being good can make you relax and become comfortable with where you are. It can breed a complacency and even an arrogance that prevents you from being open to new ideas and committed to ongoing training and skill development. Being good can prevent you from reaching the top. *Good* is the enemy of the best. Let good be part of the journey, not the destination. In which areas have you been settling for *good* instead of stretching for the best?

Action I will take today: _____

_____

JUNE 8

You can't stand still. Succeeding in sales is like climbing a ladder; you have to start at the bottom and climb up. There are several rungs along the way. A rung on a ladder, as in your career, is there to hold you just long enough to get your foot up to the next level. If you rest on the rung, it's easier to go back down than to continue up. Are you using the rungs as a launching pad to a higher point or have you been resting on them? Step up today before you start to slide back down.

Today I will: _____

_____

JUNE 9

What are your priorities each day? Daily training to develop your skills? Making follow-up calls to your customer base? Reviewing your goals? Prospecting for new customers? Do you prioritize your schedule? If you do, take it one step further. *Schedule your priorities.* Make an appointment with what's most important, just as you would make an appointment with another person. Prioritizing your schedule is a good start, scheduling your priorities has even more impact.

Strategy I will use today: _____

_____

JUNE 10

Finish your week before it begins. If you are planning each day and scheduling priorities you're on the right track. To get even more done in a week, before the week begins, do the following: write down all the activities you are going to do that week and be specific (40 calls to sold customers, 20 new prospects, 10 cold calls, meetings, training sessions, etc.) and then divide them up into the days of the week. By doing this you will begin with the whole week planned and not just one day at a time. This will give you the big picture to focus on and will keep you on track and force you to get more done. If you want to be a success, finish your day before it begins; if you want to get rich, finish your week before it begins.

Action I will take today: _____

_____

JUNE 11

Do you ever go through periods when your sales level off and become flat-lined? Our performance can become mundane, our senses dulled and our enthusiasm vanquished if we are putting all of our time into producing without increasing our capacity to do so. Increasing your capacity can include improving skills and learning new skills, installing systems or improving on existing ones, setting time aside to replenish and get into better physical and mental shape, etc. Increase your capacity and you can increase your production. What are you doing to increase your own capacity on a consistent, ongoing basis? Resist becoming so focused on production that you ignore developing the capacity to produce.

Today I will: _____

_____

JUNE 12

Are you waiting for your ship to come in? Don't hold your breath. Going to work with a lottery mindset, hoping today is that lucky day, is living in a fantasy. Your ship is more likely to come in if you do something to launch it. Nothing takes the place of definite goals, solid plans and a commitment and work ethic to attack them with every day. Waiting for something to develop or happen for you is "fool's gold." What can you do to launch, re-launch, or regain momentum, or pick up the speed of your ship today? Review the goals you set earlier in the year. Tune them up and get them on track.

Strategy I will use today: _____

_____

JUNE 13

Make sure you are doing "first things first" every day. The first things are those that bring you the greatest return on your time. They are your priorities. Resist the temptation to do unpleasant things first to get them over with, or unfinished things first–items that are left over from yesterday. The fact is that if these items are not priorities and you are not getting your greatest return from them, you shouldn't be doing them until the "first" things are complete. This takes planning and discipline but keeps you on track to producing consistent results.

Action I will take today: _____

_____

JUNE 14

Most salespeople spend more time trying to figure out shortcuts than they do spending time developing a skill. On the surface, it looks easier to take a shortcut than develop your skills. But in the long run, the more skills you develop, the less you'll want or need to shortcut your selling steps. We take shortcuts to avoid pain as we perceive it. Trying to avoid pain never made anyone well. We have to treat the cause of the pain–lack of a skill or discipline in our field. How is your personal growth plan and daily skill training coming? Remember, spend a daily minimum of 30 minutes working on product skills, selling skills and attitude and motivation. It's the cure for the need or desire to take shortcuts.

Today I will: _____

_____

JUNE 15

Are you a positive person? How do you think your co-workers, customers or family members regard you? You may be surprised. We sometimes get so bogged down and conditioned to finding fault, complaining and spewing out cynicism that we don't even notice it any more. It becomes a way of life. Staying positive is a daily discipline. It takes focus to develop and maintain it as a state of mind. We have to break our pattern of negativity and focus on what's right. Look for the good in every situation. Catch others doing something right. Take stock of yourself right now and be honest. If you were one of your co-workers, customers or family members, would what you had to say during the day be an exhilarating or debilitating experience? Do people leave your presence feeling better or worse?

Strategy I will use today: _____

JUNE
MID-MONTH ACTION PLAN

_____

_____

_____

_____

_____

_____

_____

JUNE 16

Do you have trouble with time–management? If you do, chances are good that you don't have well-defined, specific goals. The two go hand in hand. Salespeople with well-defined, specific goals know what daily activities they have to execute to stay on track to reach their goals. This makes it easier to plan their day and manage their time since they are planning around a **purpose.** Salespeople with poor time management skills most often have lost focus; their days are fractured with sporadic activity, being very busy, but not accomplishing much. If you want to be better at managing your time and priorities, set specific goals, decide on the activities you'll need to reach the goals, and use those activities as your daily compass to stay on track and get more done. Check yourself and get on track today.

Action I will take today: _____

JUNE 17

Concentrate and eliminate. Once you have set goals and determined the activities you need to reach them, it's easier to prioritize your day around your purpose. As the day goes on and things come up that demand your time and energy, examine them through the looking glass of goals you have set, and if they enhance and support them, go for it. If they do not fit into your goals and purpose; forego them. Having well-defined goals and plans sets the stage to take the numerous opportunities in a day and put them through a litmus test of sorts. It gives you a framework to evaluate and to concentrate on the activities that will help you achieve your purpose and eliminate those that would get you off track or divert your focus.

Today I will: _____

JUNE 18

When you begin to understand how long-term planning and goal setting impacts your career and life, you will see how it is easy to overestimate what you can accomplish in a day, week or month, and underestimate what you can accomplish in a year. Breaking your big picture down into daily segments keeps you focused and on the path to achieving your goals through good and bad days alike. It develops a strength of purpose and consistency that, over time, returns exponential results. As you begin to get more out of each day, look ahead to the bigger picture of the future by planning by the week and the month. As your planning discipline develops, you can apply the daily principles you've mastered into longer range planning for even greater results. Look for opportunities to begin planning with a bigger picture in mind.

Strategy I will use today: _____

JUNE 19

Daily evaluation of your goals and in making progress toward them will also help your attitude. You can't help but have a better outlook when you feel you are in control of your destiny and have a plan to get you there. It breeds a daily confidence and fulfills an important sense of daily purpose. Days start to mean more as you see them fitting into the big picture and not just being another blurb on the screen of your life. Following your plan plants positive seeds in your mind every day. When planting positive seeds in your mind, it's tougher for the weeds to get in there and take root. How can you continue to improve your attitude by improving your daily performance? Continue to search for ways. It's the key to making each day your masterpiece.

Action I will take today: _____

_____

JUNE 20

Be determined, yet flexible. When following your plans, it's important to be determined and focused on getting to where you want to be. It's also just as important to maintain a certain flexibility. Determination without flexibility results in a stubbornness akin to walking into a wall over and over again in your attempt to get through it, rather than standing back and looking a little to the right and finding a door that will take you to the other side. Maintain flexibility. Evaluate some areas where you have become "set in your ways." Could this lack of flexibility be causing you to miss opportunities and stunt your personal growth?

Today I will: _____

_____

JUNE 21

Join the marathon. Becoming proficient at setting and reaching goals and managing your time doesn't happen overnight. Achieving these things will have a profoundly positive impact on your career and your life and, like most significant accomplishments, takes time. Be patient and cut yourself some slack as you develop these new habits. When you fall short and fail, simply ask yourself what you can learn from it. *Transforming your career is a marathon, not a sprint.* Approaching it as such will make you more disciplined and focused on long term results and less impulsive and frustrated when things don't always fall the way you'd like them to. Recommit to "being in it for the long haul." Keep your eyes on the horizon and that's where you'll find your focus, as well.

Strategy I will use today: _____

_____

JUNE 22

Peer pressure can kill your career. As you begin to develop yourself and advance, it's typical that some people you work with may try to bring you back down to their level. Misery loves company. No one wants to look bad. Don't let peer pressure divert your focus. While it's desirable to have favorable relations with those you work with, somewhere along the line it may become necessary to decide if you are there to be liked or to make a living. As you advance and improve, do so with class and with an absence of arrogance. At the same time, don't ever allow anyone to reduce your goals, your drive, your vision, or your ambition to their own comfort zone. Be an example for them to follow.

Action I will take today: _____

_____

JUNE 23

Success is a daily thing, not a destination thing. Daily practice to develop and refine your skills is a discipline. Develop your own personal practice system. It has to work for you. It must be consistent, effective and attainable. Your own personal practice and training separates you from the average salesperson. Most salespeople dream of achieving worthy accomplishments. A select few stay awake and actually do them. Evaluate your personal practice system today. Is it enough? Can you stretch it?

Today I will: _____

_____

JUNE 24

There is a new monthly expense you need to add to your budget. It's hard to figure out exactly what it costs you, so leave the amount blank–you probably don't want to know the magnitude of the amount anyway. The liability being referred to is procrastination. Waiting costs money. It's often easier to wait than to actually do what you're supposed to do. It's easier to take the easy wrong than the hard right. What have you been putting off? Postponing action is postponing achievement.

Strategy I will use today: _____

_____

JUNE 25

Use your weapons. Once you begin development of a skill you have to keep on using it to make it stronger. It's like a muscle. The more you use it the stronger it gets. Leave it idle and it becomes flabby and useless. Too many salespeople learn bits and pieces of skills and then go on to another skill and then another. You're better off to have the total use and benefit of one good skill than fragments of many. Learn a skill, use it and master it. The true value of any new skill will be in direct proportion to the frequency of use. Which partial skills do you need to polish up today?

Action I will take today: _____

_____

JUNE 26

Winning is the key. The top pros in sales realize they get paid for results, not best efforts. If all that mattered was how you played the game and not the outcome of the game, we wouldn't even bother to keep score. It's great to work long and hard. It's great to put forth a superior effort. It's even better to win. If you are long on best efforts and short on results, re-look at those efforts. Are they the most effective path to where you need to go? Should something be added on the journey? Should something be deleted or fine-tuned? Constant evaluations of what you are doing and the ensuing results keep you moving to the next level. Are there any areas where you have been confusing best efforts with results?

Today I will: _____

_____

JUNE 27

When negotiating, always keep the end in mind. Too many salespeople negotiate without a clearly defined desired objective. They get too hung up on the means to get to the end. Focus on the end. Keep the means flexible and creativity will ensue. Don't get so locked into technique that you miss a desired result. This will cause you to miss potential solutions. Stay focused on the result. Keep the end in mind and the best means makes itself available to you.

Strategy I will use today: _____

_____

JUNE 28

When negotiating, your job is to manage the perceptions of the customer. You send strong signals influencing that perception by the numbers you present and how you present them in a negotiation. If you are coming down on price, come down in odd numbers, numbers that don't look like they are full of fluff. Each time you come down, do so in smaller, diminishing amounts until there is nowhere left to go. If you do come down, get a concession from the customer as well. Gain credibility by making them give you something for your price concession. (For example, get the promise of a referral, future business, etc.)

Action I will take today: _____

_____

JUNE 29

Determine their deadline. When negotiating, determine the deadline of your customer without revealing yours. Most resolutions come at the end of one party's deadline. If your customer knows you have to have the sale by the end of the month, you are at his mercy. If you know that an incentive the customer wants to take advantage of is about to disappear, you have an advantage and can hold a strong line until the end. Knowledge is power in negotiation and the more you can find out about their position, the bigger advantage you will have.

Today I will: _____

_____

JUNE 30

Slow down the process. When negotiations aren't going well, slow them down. Ask more questions. Don't be so quick to totally understand the other party's offer. Ask them to explain certain aspects, even if you know what is meant. This will help create a momentum shift and give you a chance to regroup and avoid being swept away in the customer's current.

Strategy I will use today: _____

_____

June
Month-End Action Plan

_____

_____

_____

_____

_____

_____

_____

_____

_____

_____

_____

_____

_____

_____

July 1

Become a better evaluator. The difference between average and the top sales professionals is the evaluations they make: evaluations of situations, customers, obstacles and opportunities. Better evaluations lead to better solutions. If someone is excelling in an area you are not, it may mean they are making better evaluations in that area. Check your criteria for evaluating. Is it covering all the angles? Is it thorough enough? Does it take the necessary time to deduce correct action? Are you in a *productive or a survival* state of mind when making evaluations? What can you add to your evaluation criteria to make it more effective?

Action I will take today: _____

_____

July 2

Are you stealing? If you are not pushing yourself to your limits every day in pursuit of excellence you are stealing from your employer, your family and yourself. Nobody hired you to pace your performance or to budget your efforts to suffice as enough to get by. Every day is a challenge to prove yourself all over again. Yesterday, good or bad, doesn't matter–so quit thinking about it and living in it. Mediocrity is a rut. Stay in it long enough and it turns into a grave. Decide to pick up the pace starting today. Push yourself!

Today I will: _____

_____

July 3

Mediocre performance is brought on by mediocre thinking. Change it. You can't solve today's challenges and problems at the same level of thinking you were at when you created them. Go to work on your skills, habits and attitudes every day. This will keep you out of a comfort zone. A well known writer once observed that habit can be the best servant or the worst master. Professional skills, habits and attitudes produce professional compensation. Are you working to improve all three of these areas daily? What are your specific plans to do so today?

Strategy I will use today: _____

_____

JULY 4

Break them! If you have techniques and systems that have worked consistently for you in the past, but have brought you to a leveling off period in performance more recently, break them! Foolish consistency is not a virtue. Winston Churchill said he'd rather be right than consistent. Constantly reevaluate the areas critical to your success and make improvements and adjustments as often as necessary. When you keep yourself in a box, you put your career in a casket. What's the number one change you know you need to make that you've put off long enough? Commit to an immediate action towards changing it–right now! Then look for the next area where you can do some breaking. Repeat the process.

Action I will take today: _____

_____

JULY 5

Practice! Every professional overachiever in sales must develop their own personal practice system; one that goes far beyond the standard and required training meetings and sessions routinely attended. Those serve a purpose, but even the average people in your organization go to those. *Your* system must take your personal growth and development to the next level. It must be consistent, effective and it must work for you. Continually developing your skills and refining your approach take you to the top in sales. Start your own personal practice system and constantly look for ways to upgrade it. Remember, everyone goes to training meetings. It's what you do in between the training meetings that will take you above the crowd.

Today I will: _____

_____

JULY 6

Plant the seeds and the harvest will take care of itself. Too many salespeople are focused primarily on their daily harvest of sales. While the need for daily sales success is important, a day should be judged by the seeds planted more than the harvest gained. Continual harvests without new seeds for sales being planted will ultimately turn into an empty crop. Planting consistently will provide continual harvests and feasts. What is your plan for planting seeds today? For the week? The month?

Strategy I will use today: _____

_____

JULY 7

Plant in your mind as well. Speaking of seeds, what seeds have you been planting in your mind? Failing to continually plant positive seeds in your mind allows the weeds of neglect to take root. Plant often and plenty and you'll reap often and plenty. Plant little, reap little. Plant nothing, reap disaster. Feed your attitude a daily feast of positive thoughts, ideas and affirmations that will keep the locusts at bay. Locusts are in the area–negative people, situations, stumbling blocks and setbacks–always looking for an opening. Only constant attention and prevention will keep them from beginning their siege.

Action I will take today: _____

_____

JULY 8

Quit blaming mom and dad. Too many salespeople blame and justify what they do and why they do it. While your circumstances and background may have influenced who you are, you are ultimately responsible for what you become. Quit blaming your boss or fellow workers. It's your decisions and not your conditions that determine your performance. It is your responsibility to be responsible. In fact, the most important ability you have is responsibility. There is a power that comes with accepting responsibility for your actions and your status. This power allows you to point yourself forward, move on and focus while others are pointing the finger. Begin a more serious accountability mindset today.

Today I will: _____

_____

JULY 9

Many salespeople are great "idea" people. They have lots of suggestions and ideas as to how things should be done or can be made better. Idea people are not particularly impressive. Anyone standing in a hot shower long enough can walk away with an idea. Salespeople who can implement ideas and take them from the theoretical stage to the action stage are in demand. They make it happen. They are a far cry from that group who would rather study the race than ever join the race, endlessly discussing and never deciding anything. Which ideas are you carrying around in your mind that need to be turned into action? What are you waiting for?

Strategy I will use today: _____

_____

JULY 10

Do you have momentum? It's a daily thing. It's brought on and sustained by a consistent flow of productive activities such as learning, practicing, drilling, prospecting, following up, planning and goal setting. A freight train traveling at 55 mph can break through a five foot thick concrete wall and never miss a beat. That same train, while immobile on the track, can be kept immobile by a one inch square block of wood. Keep moving. Keep planting. Keep learning. You'll keep earning. What are you doing on an ongoing basis to sustain your momentum?

Action I will take today: _____

_____

JULY 11

Pats on the back make you feel good, but they seldom teach you much. You learn and grow through reflective feedback and constructive critique. Too few salespeople seek this out however. We want the strokes, the kudos. Critique can hurt our ego. We take it personally. We resent it. This is unfortunate. If you can grasp the fact that feedback pushes you out of mediocrity and toward new heights you will welcome it. You'll even seek it out. The next time you hear criticism, try something different– listen. Listen with an open mind and closed mouth. See what you can learn and how you can improve.

Today I will: _____

_____

JULY 12

Ideas are energy. If you feel worn out or used up, seek out new ideas. They energize you. They pick you up and make you think. They can get the juices flowing again. Salespeople who are in ruts have stopped seeking out new ideas, new angles and fresh perspectives. Read. Listen to tapes. Seek out other's opinions. They are stimulating. Next time you're short on energy or feel a little groggy, pass on the extra cup of coffee and go find some new ideas. Then turn them into action!

Strategy I will use today: _____

_____

JULY 13

Ideas are energy and so is vision. Having a clear vision of what you want to do, where you want to be and how you want to feel is invigorating. Too often we get so caught up in today that today bores us, wears us out and fails to stimulate. A solid and exciting vision keeps you focused on the big picture. It keeps you going. It gets you past the small stuff that can get blown out of proportion when you can't see further than this moment. Vision invigorates and preserves you. Lack of vision wears you down. As stated in Proverbs, "Where there is no vision, the people perish." What is your vision? Is it big enough to cause you to do something different than you would do without it?

Action I will take today: _____

_____

JULY 14

See if these quotes can help your purpose and vision. It's been said that we make a living by what we get, but we make a life by what we give. Albert Schweitzer said, "The purpose of human life is to serve, and to show compassion and the will to help others." Danny Thomas observed, "All of us are born for a reason, but all of us don't discover why. Success in life has nothing to do with what you gain in life or accomplish for yourself. It's what you do for others." Zig Ziglar added, "You can have everything in life that you want if you help enough other people get what they want." Puts a new perspective on your job, doesn't it?

Today I will: _____

_____

JULY 15

Warranty or guarantee? Your future has neither. Your track record and past accomplishments assure nothing. The future of your career is up for grabs. This should not cause anxiety, but an anxious burn to get busy. You get to fill in the blanks for your future. What you do or don't do today starts the process for tomorrow. To determine your future, take a good look at the decisions you are making today, because where you are right now is a result of decisions you made yesterday. Want to be someplace better tomorrow? Start by making better decisions today!

Strategy I will use today: _____

_____

JULY
MID-MONTH ACTION PLAN

_____

_____

_____

_____

_____

_____

JULY 16

You're not a houseplant. No one is going to come along and water you, repot you, or pull off your dead spots. Growth is your responsibility. Your supervisor or manager is responsible _to_ you but not _for_ you. What have you been leaving up to your supervisors that you can take more responsibility for?

Action I will take today: _____

_____

JULY 17

Are you busy? It could be a good or a bad thing. Some salespeople think that "busyness" is the thing to be. We can get so caught up doing reactionary tasks that we fail to do what is most important. It's the old adage of sacrificing the important for the urgent. Take a good look at your busy days. What are you really accomplishing, if anything? Are your most important activities being subordinated to the fire drill of the moment? The best cure is to continue to schedule your priorities and keep them as you would any other appointment. If something urgent does come up and get them off track, you're more likely to reschedule the important activity–not forget about it.

Today I will: _____

_____

July 18

Have a weekly reconnection with your planned activities and evaluate how close you are to being on track and determine where you fell short. Then take corrective action to get back on the track toward your goals. This will stop you from drifting too far off course and winding up going in circles, or worse yet, descending into a rut. It's easier to stay closer to shore when the current starts pulling you out to sea if you take an occasional look over your shoulder and can determine when to start swimming back to where you need to be.

Strategy I will use today: _____

July 19

Are you crisp? Precise, enthusiastic and fluent presentations earn confidence from your prospect, customer and future client. This comes through preparation. On the other hand, sloppy, staggering verbal expressions indicate a sloppy thought process. This comes from winging it. Sloppy practice habits portend sloppy performance. You can't hide it. You can't fool the customer. You end up standing naked and exposed before your customer. Make sure you're in shape.

Action I will take today: _____

July 20

Laugh with your customers. Humor sells. Not silly, nonsensical humor. But a light, relevant humor. Humor relaxes and helps establish common ground with your customer. It makes you a real person. So laugh a little with your customer. If you can't smile, grin. If you can't grin, keep out of the way until you can. Smiles sell.

Today I will: _____

July 21

Take your time off. Overloading yourself dulls your senses and diminishes your effectiveness. Replenish. Relax. You may think you can't afford to take the time away. You may be worried by what it will cost. What you can't calculate is the cost of *not* doing it. There may never be a *good* time to take your day off or your vacation so you may as well take it as you earn it. In your rise above the crowd you will need to implement replenishing patterns in your life. Are your current patterns adequate?

Strategy I will use today: _____

_____

JULY 22

Slow down. Get *this* next moment right. Hastiness will dilute your concentration. It will disrupt your schedule, confuse your priorities and prohibit you from maintaining the consistency you need to excel at sales. Slowing down with purpose increases concentration and focus. Where are you rushing? What could it be costing you? What can you do to slow it down?

Action I will take today: _____

_____

JULY 23

Watch your words. Watch what you say. Watch how you say them. Watch when you say them. Know when to say nothing at all. Sometimes the best close is knowing when to keep quiet. Don't feel obligated to fill every quiet moment with verbiage. Silence always means something, but it is not always a cue for you to speak. Become more aware of your words. Don't keep rattling them off in an automatic manner. Your words either elevate or devastate your chances of making the sale. Dizzy Gillepsie once said, "It took me all my life to learn the biggest music lesson of all–what not to play." Don't let it take your whole career to figure it out.

Today I will: _____

_____

JULY 24

Replace your open door with a screen door. You need time in your day for short- and long-term planning, creative thinking and the completion of meaningful selling activities. Constant interruptions by phone and in person from family, friends, associates in the business, fellow employees and even old customers can grind your daily productivity down to nothing. Limit calls you take from friends and family as well as associates in the business. It is estimated that each call you take lasts an average of twelve minutes whereas each call you plan and make averages only seven minutes. Saving five minutes per phone call on a dozen calls per day buys you back an hour of your time--and this is only the beginning of the time you can save if you'll pay more attention to where you're spending it. For a couple of days, keep track of how many times the phone is in your hand and how many times someone just walks into your office for conversation. It will shock you and motivate you to get serious about replacing your open door with a screen door.

Today I will: _____

_____

July 25

Having a hard time closing deals lately? Go back and take a look at the rapport, or lack of it, that you had during the last deal you lost. One of the keys to selling is rapport. In fact, rapport can be your best means to gain influence with people. It's the ability to initiate and quickly build a relationship based on trust and mutual understanding. Rapport is common ground. It's showing you care. It attracts people to you and makes them want to deal with you. It creates the comfort and trust necessary to make doing business with you a wise and safe choice. When you get off track in selling, go back to the basics and slow it down. Build rapport and the rest of the process flows easier and has a happier ending. What are some rapport building questions and observations that you have in your selling arsenal? What can you do to improve them?

Strategy I will use today: _____

_____

July 26

Rest. Recharge. Replenish. Tired salespeople tend to dwell on problems longer. They become more negative. They take shortcuts. They lose their zest and motivation for what they do. The list of penalties for not keeping this physical and mental balance goes on and on. The quiet time you spend with yourself; resting, reflecting, planning, meditating and relaxing helps equip you for the busy times. It aids you in peaking your performance. Long-term success in sales is all about balance. How are these areas balanced in your life: work, play, family, spiritual, physical? If you find yourself a little bit out of whack, force yourself to spend some quiet time to get things back on track. Use rest to refocus, replenish and recharge. The sooner you restore balance to your life and career, the sooner you will reach the top–and you'll be more equipped to stay there once you do. What have you done to tweak your recharging and replenishing patterns?

Action I will take today: _____

_____

JULY 27

Want to improve your output? Improve your input. Want to change where you are? Change what you are putting into your mind. Want life to be easier on you? Then be tougher on yourself. Want to get everything you want in life? Then help enough other people get what they want and you will. Want to be able to do the things you want to do when you want to do them? Then start doing the things you ought to do when you ought to do them. Do you have a past you're less than thrilled with? Don't sweat it, tomorrow is a clean slate. Zig Ziglar has done a great job of putting all of the above statements into perspective for us. They make you think. They make sense and they work. If you haven't read a book by Zig in a while–or ever–it's time to do it. You need better input to produce better output. Let Zig help you change your thinking and get you to the top and above the crowd. See the recommended reading list at the back of the book for suggested books by Zig.

Today I will: _____

_____

JULY 28

Have you committed to the balance we talked about a couple of days ago? You can take it a step further by figuring in some time for wellness. Eating the wrong foods and lack of proper exercise can do more than eventually kill you. It can kill your career on the way to killing you. Not paying attention to your wellness drains your energy. It stifles your creativity and productivity. It can hurt your self-esteem and impede your confidence. How much money have you ever made while lying sick in bed? How many memorable moments have you spent with your family while lying sick in bed? You don't have to be in the gym every day and eat all your meals at a salad bar to look and feel better and enjoy improved health. It can be as simple as making better daily choices and implementing a small daily discipline to get you going. If you don't take time for wellness you'll have no choice but to take time for illness. You get to choose.

Strategy I will use today: _____

_____

July 29

Do you have a survival attitude or a conceding attitude? A survival attitude is developed as a learned behavior. It is built up every time you decide to persist when it might be easier to concede and give up. It is strengthened as you fight your way through adversity–bad days, weeks or months, personal or professional tragedy. The actions you build it with become a habit–a positive reflex in the face of roadblocks. It is always easier to concede to difficulties. It's easier to rationalize away your dreams than it is to realize them. That's why it's so much easier and common for salespeople to be mediocre than it is for them to be top performing professionals. Do you have a survival attitude? Think back on how you handled the last couple of major setbacks or challenges that came your way. What will you do differently if they come around again? Start building your survival attitude at the next opportunity.

Action I will take today: _____

_____

July 30

Go and look in the mirror right now. If image is everything and a first impression sets the tone for the success of your next sale, how will you do? Sometimes we tend to relax our dress and grooming standards. We have bad mornings. We get in a hurry. Sometimes we start out the day looking crisp and sharp and then regress as it wears on. You can't afford to do that any longer. A successful image and professional first impression make a lasting impact. Regardless of how much you know, some people will never be able to get past that first image of you. What you are will speak so loudly they won't be able to hear what you are saying. Make sure what you are is what you ought to be–from the start of the day to the finish. Don't let your guard down in appearance, language or attitude. A good first impression creates momentum. A bad one sinks your ship; whether it's 6:00 a.m. or 11:00 p.m.

Today I will: _____

_____

JULY 31

How many times during the day do you feel hungry? Most people feel hungry for a meal right around breakfast, lunch, supper and again right before they go to bed at night. How many times during the day do you feel hungry for a sale and for success? Not hungry because you "have to have a sale," but because your inner desire and drive is burning to get one? If we were as hungry as often and as intensely for success as we are for food during a day our sales would probably triple! How do you develop hunger? It starts with a clearly defined set of goals and purpose that keep you moving in the right direction. What specific purposes are moving you today? What goals are causing you to go the extra mile? What force is creating your consuming hunger for more? Are you lacking that burning hunger? Then set bigger goals. Demand more of yourself. Get moving toward something bigger! Now!

Strategy I will use today: _____

_____

JULY
MONTH-END ACTION PLAN

_____

_____

_____

_____

_____

_____

_____

August 1

Are you a weather vane or a compass? Too many salespeople act like weather vanes. Whichever way the wind is blowing, whatever seems to be the latest fad or quick fix, wherever they see the greenest grass pop up is the direction in which they head. Like most weather vanes, these salespeople end up going in circles and wind up their careers in about the same place they started. Salespeople who act as a compass encounter all of the turbulence in their careers as well. They just don't let it get them off track. True north is still true north regardless of what is going on around them. Their direction is clear. They may stop to pause for awhile, even taking a step back so they can take two forward. Their purpose and goals keep them going. That keeps them grounded to what they have to do to and makes them less susceptible to distractions, detractions and all of the unproductive energy leaks on their way to success. Set your compass on true north. It makes it easier to focus on and arrive at where you need to end up when the storms start.

Action I will take today: _____

_____

August 2

"Average" is your enemy. Author John Mason shares the following thoughts in his book, *An Enemy Called Average:*

- Don't ever start your day in neutral
- You can't get ahead while trying to get even
- What you set your heart on will determine how you spend your life
- The best time of the day is now
- Nothing dies quicker than a new idea in a closed mind
- The key to your future is hidden in your daily approach to life

How can you use these thoughts to get more out of each day? How can you use them to propel you past the mass of average in the selling profession and into the top levels of income and success? As Mason says, "Put mediocrity and unfulfilled dreams where they belong...out of your life."

Today I will: _____

_____

August 3

How's your image as a professional salesperson? Is it where you want to be? It shouldn't be. You should always be expecting more and striving towards becoming more. Set a bigger, broader, more successful image of yourself and then go to work to make up the difference. This keeps you going. It keeps you out of ruts and comfort zones. Focus on growing internally to reach that higher external image you have of yourself. In order for your external world to grow larger, your internal capacity and image must grow larger. What are you doing on a daily basis to get bigger on the inside?

Strategy I will use today: _____

_____

AUGUST 4

What type of movie would you make? Would you be willing to have someone tape your daily routine and use it as a training tape for others in your field? Could they record your phone conversations, tape your presentations and capture what you do in between deals? What type of training film would it be? What would people be willing to pay for it? The fact is that what you are being paid is a direct reflection of what your tape would be worth. Make the tape worth more and you'll be worth more. What two key areas would you want to be on the tape? What four key areas would you want to improve before it became part of your training tape legacy?

Action I will take today: _____

_____

AUGUST 5

Are you using band-aid cures for terminal sales sicknesses? Persistence and the right sales behavior are important. Attitude and motivation is vital as well. But neither of these is enough to maximize performance in selling. Working on persistence and behavior can help you move more quickly and efficiently–to the wrong place. Attitude and motivation can get you so psyched up that you don't even realize or care that you've arrived in the wrong spot. The key is the right map. The right plan. The right skills, habits and attitudes all built around the right purpose and end. You wouldn't use a band-aid to try and cure cancer in your body. So stop trying to use them to fix your career. Check your map and make sure it's what it should be.

Today I will: _____

_____

August 6

Don't let the "grave-diggers" bring you down. Every organization has them. The fault finders. The cynics and complainers. The group that would rather study the race than join the race. The group that would rather discuss than decide. They will resent your success. They will find excuses as to why you are more successful than they. They will rationalize away their mediocrity and can cause high achievers much frustration. Don't let them. Unfortunately, these people are everywhere. The important thing is to be able to identify them and then have as little to do with them as possible. Don't let any of their mental and verbal garbage cloud your picture. As Einstein said, "Great spirits will always encounter violent opposition from mediocre minds." Who are the grave-diggers in your organization that you need to avoid?

Strategy I will use today: _____

_____

August 7

Grave-diggers have a scarcity mentality. They don't want anyone to get anything that they don't have. They're afraid if someone gets something special such as a bonus, a promotion, a new account, that it means that somehow there will be less left for them. Achievers in sales have an abundance mentality. They know that there is plenty to go around to those who work hard, have a plan, focus on results, give 110% and continually do the right thing. Which mentality do you have? Shift your mindset from scarcity to abundance and you'll find more than enough.

Action I will take today: _____

_____

August 8

Want to perform better? Practice better. There is no shortcut. Sales trainer Tom Hopkins said, "Anything you choose to do in life, you'll only be as good as you are in the practice drill." Great coaches know that the game is played in a stadium, but it's won or lost on the practice field. It goes back to improving your output by improving your input. If you want more output, increase the input–of practice, drilling and rehearsing. It's simple in concept. It's tougher in application. It's not a secret to success. There is no secret to it. Many people know exactly what they need to do to improve. Very few actually get serious enough to just do it.

Today I will: _____

_____

AUGUST 9

Have you started your conscious effort to stay away from grave-diggers in your life? If you have any doubt about the importance of with whom you associate, consider these quotes: "Show me a person's friends and I'll show you their character"–Ed Cole, Men's Movement Leader. "My choice to change my closest friends was a turning point in my life"–John Mason, best-selling author. "Your accomplishments do not make you great, it's your friends"–Norman Schwarzkoph, retired U.S. General. Take an inventory of your best friends and closest associates. Do they move you toward where you want to go?

Strategy I will use today: _____

_____

AUGUST 10

Explode into today! No "ho-hum." Make something happen! Take action steps toward your top goals. If you came into work today to wait for something to happen, change your mindset. There is no reason today can't be a masterpiece. The hardest part is getting started. Write down the three top things you want to accomplish today and focus on them until they are done. Create your own momentum! No more idling in neutral. Explode! It's habit-forming! It's a habit that will bring you to new levels and it can all start right now!! Explode into those three activities which you write down, and don't look back!

Action I will take today: _____

_____

AUGUST 11

Stay true! Once you set goals that you can believe in and develop plans that motivate you to daily action, once you are on the right track to creating the discipline and habits necessary to get you there, stay true! Don't keep reinventing yourself. Remain focused, yet flexible. Alter your approach and improve it whenever you can, but don't keep reinventing "you;" develop "you." Keep working on "you." But don't keep on reinventing "you." It will cloud your focus, distort your purpose and kill your momentum.

Today I will: _____

_____

AUGUST 12

Is your memory selective? Too many salespeople only remember their old customers when they need them again for more business or for referrals. It's a selective memory process that is as transparent and weak as its motives. Customer relations is a two way street. Initiating a relationship with a customer or prospect is important, but maintaining it on a mutually beneficial basis is vital. Contact your customer base regularly, by phone and by mail. (Avoid the temptation to contact them only when you want something.) Keep them informed. Let them know you are thinking about them. Remind them that you are there for them when they need you. Think of your relationship with the customers you have as wholly reciprocal. You do your part and they'll come through when you need them.

Strategy I will use today: _____

_____

AUGUST 13

Are you willing to pay the price? So many people in sales resign themselves to average careers because they just don't think they have it. More often than not it's not a matter of not having it. It's a matter of not wanting to pay the price to get it. It's too easy to settle for average in this business. We can sugarcoat our excuses until eternity but it won't change the hard facts that most people know what they need to do, have resources available to them, can get all of the help they need if they'd ask for it, but still won't because it's easier not to. There is a price to pay for success in this business and the great equalizer is that you get exactly what you pay for. Have you been paying enough?

Action I will take today: _____

_____

AUGUST 14

Start over! If you don't like how your year has been going so far, start it over today. You don't have to wait until New Year's Day for a fresh start with a new set of resolutions. Too many salespeople get caught up in the year as if it's a current that they can't swim against or get out of. So they just ride it out until the next week, next month, next quarter or next year. Draw the line, reset your focus and start over today. It's refreshing. It builds new momentum and puts the past where it needs to be...far behind you.

Today I will: _____

_____

AUGUST 15

Selling skills, habits and attitudes are important. So are product knowledge and a solid customer base. So here's an easy question. How do you rate when it comes to dealing with people? Too many salespeople are very good at the technical aspects of their job but lack the people skills needed to get them to the highest levels of selling success. The Stanford Research Institute found that the money you make in any endeavor is determined to be only 12.5% by the knowledge you have and 87.5% by your ability to deal effectively with people. John D. Rockefeller once said that he'd pay more for the ability to deal with people than any other ability under the sun. What are your weaknesses in dealing with people and how can you improve them? What are your strengths and what can you do to make them better?

Strategy I will use today: _____

AUGUST
MID-MONTH ACTION PLAN

_____

_____

_____

_____

_____

AUGUST 16

Short-term failures are here to stay in sales. Try as we may to avoid/eliminate them, they are a fact of life. Long range goals stop you from being frustrated by the short-term failures as they come up. They keep the "big picture" on your mind and in front of you. That's why the most frustrated and miserable people in sales are the ones without the long range perspective to get them through the short-term speed bumps. Want to reduce your frustrations, have more fun, keep more focus and enjoy more success? Develop and then constantly improve upon the long-range goals you need to get past today. You can cmpower yourself today with solid goals for tomorrow.

Action I will take today: _____

_____

AUGUST 17

Are you inspired? If so, are you willing to perspire to follow your inspiration? If not, your inspiration is just another good intention or more "pie in the sky." If you are willing to perspire, great! Is your perspiration fueled by inspiration? If not, get ready to beat your head against the wall. Inspiration without perspiration is a daydream. Perspiration without inspiration is a nightmare. You need both ingredients together. Do yours match up?

Today I will: _____

_____

AUGUST 18

Speaking of good intentions, are you still talking about all the things you are going to accomplish "tomorrow?" Chances are you did the same thing yesterday. Take a look at the action you committed to take on March 2nd. How are you doing? What things can you stop talking about and start taking action toward doing today? Isn't it time to get serious and put your money where your mouth is?

Strategy I will use today: _____

_____

AUGUST 19

When you attend training sessions and meetings do you consider them an event? They aren't. Training is a process. It never ends. You are never trained. To think that your training is complete is to believe that you can no longer improve. It is to resign yourself to the fact that whatever level you are at now is as good as it gets. Change your mindset to see training as a process and you will keep your approach open to positive change, keep your mind open to constant improvements and be on the lookout for steps you can take forward on a daily basis.

Action I will take today: _____

_____

AUGUST 20

One of the surest ways to rise above the crowd and secure success for a lifetime is committing to improve yourself in some way, every day. When speaking of Sam Walton, Wal-Mart executive Bill Glass remarked that he could not remember a day in his life when Sam didn't improve himself in some way. How about you? What did you do to improve yourself last month? Last week? Yesterday? What will you do today? Sam Walton started improving himself each day long *before* he became one of the richest men in the world, not after. What can you learn from his example? Life is not just going to come along and improve you. You have to consciously develop and improve yourself.

Today I will: _____

_____

AUGUST 21

Are you a lone wolf? Going it alone up the success ladder can be an isolated process. In fact, it's been said that if you can accomplish your plans by yourself, your plans are too small. Surround yourself with a mastermind of driven, positive and achievement-oriented colleagues and friends. There is power in the synergy and support of like-minded associates. Mother Teresa once said, "I can do what you can't do and you can do what I can't do: together we can do great things." Don't let pride, arrogance or selfishness prevent you from contributing to the success of others and accepting their assistance toward your own success journey.

Strategy I will use today: _____

_____

AUGUST 22

Are you giving up on deals too soon? If so, chances are that you're not working hard enough or working smart enough to put those deals together. Vince

Lombardi once said that the harder you work, the harder it is to surrender. Once you put all you have into a deal and get out of the habit of treating it as just another "idea," it'll become harder to accept the fact that it won't go together. This will push you to new heights of creativity and determination to see it through to completion. What can you do to turn up the hunger and intensity you have for selling up to the next notch?

Action I will take today: _____

AUGUST 23

Too many salespeople embrace success. They spend more time patting themselves on the back than they do refocusing on the next objective. It's fine to enjoy your success, but do not dwell on it. It's too easy to latch onto the results of your success and forget the drive and exhausting work it took to get you there. Laziness and complacency tempt the most successful people in sales. What safeguards do you have in place to ensure you can "survive" success?

Today I will: _____

AUGUST 24

Want to be more relaxed on the job? Spend more time preparing. Want to feel less stress when you're in front of clients? Spend more time practicing. Want to have more fun at your job? Spend more time drilling. Want to be more confident in your selling career? Spend more time rehearsing. Want to get more money out of your job? Spend more time *becoming* more by working on yourself and you will. There is nothing glamorous about repetitive practice, drilling and rehearsing. There is also no substitute for developing selling skills, habits and attitudes. The road to execution is paved by repetition. Have you been doing your share? Are you doing it on a daily basis? Repetition is most effective when done consistently and not in crash course formats. What is your personal program for practice, drilling and rehearsing to move yourself to the next level in sales?

Strategy I will use today: _____

August 25

Never accept their first offer. When negotiating, to make your customers feel good, never accept their first offer. People like to feel like they've won something and when you accept their first offer you can scare them off. They'll think they're paying too much and second-guess themselves for leaving money on the table. Even if their offer is profitable and generous, don't accept it. Make them fight a little bit. Even if you wind up taking the offer, at least they'll feel like they've had their way and gained a concession from you. They'll feel better about the deal and so will you.

Action I will take today: _____

_____

August 26

Don't allow "nibbling." After a negotiation is complete and everyone is relaxed and feeling good, negotiators will often "nibble"–try for one more concession. They do this when your guard is down and you mentally have a done deal. It's tougher at this time to destroy the progress of the negotiation so we often feel benevolent and give in. Don't. Be prepared for nibbling and handle it politely, professionally and firmly. When they try for that last concession reply, "Come on, John, we both know you're getting a heck of a deal and our product is worth every dime you're investing in it. I don't blame you for trying but, seriously now, let's wrap this up and get you out of here so you can start enjoying your new (car, stereo, watch, etc.). Did you want to handle the purchase by cash or charge?" Bypass the nibble by restating the value of what they are buying, acknowledging their attempt while brushing it aside, and reclosing the deal.

Today I will: _____

_____

August 27

Bypass the impasse. When you are at an impasse in a negotiation, set aside that one item and go forward with other points you can agree on. Return to the impasse after you have made progress in the other areas and approach it again. At this point you will both have more time invested in one another and have a better feel for what needs to be done to bring the deal to a successful conclusion.

Strategy I will use today: _____

_____

August 28

Counter-punch the concession. Every time you give a concession in a negotiation, get something immediately in return. Don't get run over and try to regain lost ground later by pulling out last minute demands in an attempt to get even. Keep track of what you are giving and getting and immediately upon giving a concession, tie it to something for your side.

Action I will take today: _____

August 29

Don't get bogged down into trying to prove the other side wrong during a negotiation. You will not persuade them to your beliefs. Spend more time justifying why you have taken your position and why you deserve what you are asking for. Do a better job of justifying your wants and needs and you'll be less likely to have to give concessions to help prop up and salvage a weak case.

Today I will: _____

August 30

Watch the turf. Negotiations are more advantageous if held on your turf, where you have a psychological and strategic "one up." There are times when you may want to have a negotiation on the turf of your counterpart. This would be the case when the real decision maker is to be found on the other's turf. Whenever possible, go to where you can find, pin down and commit the "powers that be." In this manner you can close your counterpart's "check with a higher authority" escape clause.

Strategy I will use today: _____

August 31

Preparation is as big a key to negotiating as it is to everything else you do in sales. Do your homework. Find out all you can about the potential client. Their needs, wants, problems they've had with previous suppliers, the weaknesses of current suppliers, etc. You will also want to check with others who have negotiated with the client to find out their styles, methods and tendencies. The more information you can obtain, the more avenues and weapons you'll have with which to close the deal when it really counts. Time spent gaining insight and preparation is priceless in negotiations and separates the haves and the have-nots in selling.

Action I will take today:_____

AUGUST
MONTH-END ACTION PLAN

_____

_____

_____

_____

_____

_____

_____

_____

_____

_____

September 1

Step up to the plate for your customers. When it comes to telling your customers that you put them first, put your money where your mouth is. When trying to make a deal with your customer, your customer doesn't want to hear about all the reasons why you cannot do something. They want you to at least try. Go to bat for them and let them know you will. Fade some heat for your customers and get them something–even a small something–to show you mean business. Talk is cheap. While you should never promise you *will* be able to do something, you can always promise that you can *try*. Then go to work for your customer.

Action I will take today: _____

September 2

Have you been using enough questions in your sales presentation to keep things flowing? Questions keep you in control and keep the client involved in the process. Too many salespeople try to tell their way into a sale rather than question their way into it. Clients buy when their needs are met. You can't determine their needs by rambling. Find out their needs and the needs will lead to solutions. Solutions create sales.

Today I will: _____

September 3

Many salespeople are befuddled when they give a great presentation and still don't make the sale. They say, "But I told them everything about the product and they still wouldn't buy it," without realizing that that was the problem. Remember, customers have buying motives called hot buttons. Every time you talk about their hot button and how your product will serve their needs, you move them closer to the sale. Each time you mention a feature that they are indifferent to, you take a step back. Find the hot buttons–by asking, not guessing or assuming–and hit on them over and over. When you talk about what they care about you create excitement. Excitement creates urgency to buy, and you know what that creates. What are the questions you are using to determine hot buttons? How can you improve your investigating techniques to do a better job of finding their buying motives?

Strategy I will use today: _____

September 4

Finding the customer's buying motives won't do much good if you don't know enough about your product's features to cover the different interests your customer has. What do you do to study your product? Have you updated your knowledge lately? Have you identified all the major hot buttons your products elicit and do you know enough about each one to make a powerful presentation? Product knowledge is not a crash course proposition. It is an ongoing quest for turning your product's features into advantages and benefits and showing how they are superior to the competition. Learn something new about your product daily and become more convincing and authoritative in your presentations. This will breed confidence and enthusiasm that will be transferred over to your customers. Develop your own daily study program for your product. Start with the best sellers and move on to cover your whole line.

Action I will take today: _____

_____

September 5

There are five major motivators that prompt customers to buy. Understanding these five areas and how you can use them will lead you to connecting better with your customers and subsequently making more sales. The first area is *gain*. Customers want to gain something, not just buy something. It is your job to clearly spell out what is to be gained by this purchase. How will it change things? What will it add to the quality of the customer's life or business? What positive effect will the product have and in what areas? Clearly show that the purchase is a step forward and you build momentum that leads to an easier sale. Show the gain. Show it clearly and show it in every conceivable area.

Today I will: _____

_____

September 6

The second motivator of the five major motivators you must recognize is *pain*. When a customer makes a new purchase, it means something will have to change. Customers may resist this change and be tempted to stick with the way things are because they are more comfortable with the present scenario than they are with the prospects of changing it. Your job is to show greater pain in maintaining the status quo than in not making a purchase. You should also show the pain that will follow by making the mistake of purchasing a competitor's product. Create a fear of loss. Skillfully arouse the awareness of the pain that will be involved with not making the best decision–buying your product. Gently prove your case as to why your solution erases the pain and replaces it with pleasure.

Strategy I will use today: _____

_____

September 7

The third of the major motivators is pleasure. Customers make purchases to reach new levels of satisfaction, convenience, pride, comfort and enjoyment. You succeed in selling your product when you raise the value of what you are selling equal to or past the price of attaining the sought-after pleasure. Paint mental ownership and talk in terms throughout your presentation as though they already have bought your product. "Paint" them into the pleasure of ownership and they won't want to give it back.

Action I will take today: _____

_____

September 8

The fourth of the major motivators is pride. Customers buy to satisfy their own egos and to obtain recognition and approval from those around them. They often make purchases to assert their self-esteem and reward themselves for their achievements in life. Painting mental ownership that appeals to their pride is a powerful trigger for emotional buying. Selling to pride helps take some of the analytical logic out of those who would drag out a decision, and gives them the reason they need to talk themselves into doing it now. Appealing to this force will be the cause for many impulsive closes, because pride triggers emotion and erases logic.

Today I will: _____

_____

September 9

The fifth major motivator is peace of mind. Customers want to feel assured in their decision. They want to avoid the uneasiness that uncertainty brings. This is an impacting force in selling insurance and related instruments. Customers want security, protection and the clear conscience that comes with knowing they aren't being careless with their loved ones, associates or themselves. When you appeal to this motivator, they will pay to have the fire put out and to regain their sense of self-assuredness.

Strategy I will use today: _____

_____

September 10

Are you going to meet your customers' expectations today? In a more competitive and precise buying and selling market, consumers have come to expect more from sales professionals. With increased competition for available dollars, consumers expect to deal with someone who looks, sounds and acts like a professional. They want answers and demand service. Do you look, sound and act the part of what they are looking for? Remember that more often than not your competition is not the other product or service as much as it is the other sales professional. Are you up to winning the battle today? What edge do you have? What additional angles can you work on to hone your approach and complete your advantage?

Action I will take today: _____

_____

September 11

Do you have a "big picture?" You cannot put the pieces of a successful career together without one. Think of your career "big picture" as a jigsaw puzzle. Before you would try to put a jigsaw puzzle together you'd have to look at the picture of the finished product intently and refer to it numerous times to keep you on track as you constructed the puzzle. The big picture in your career might be a position, an income or a territory. If you have a clear picture of it, the path to get there will become clear also. With a blurry or sloppy picture of where you are headed, the path will be blurry and sloppy as well. What is your big picture? Can you define it clearly? Is it written down as a goal? Do you refer to it often? If you get close to reaching it, is there another, grander picture in line to take its place?

Today I will: _____

_____

SEPTEMBER 12

Quit rationalizing away the sales you miss. Stop making excuses to try and make yourself feel better. The next time you miss or lose a deal, ask yourself what you can learn from it before you rush to defend your performance or excuse your lack of success. If you can learn something and incorporate that knowledge into the next proposal you will never feel that you have wasted time with a customer. The time may not have paid off this time but it is an investment in future sales. Think about the last three customers you worked and sold nothing to. What could you do differently next time to move them closer to the sale? Do a "post-mortem" on each and every deal. It's like a sports team watching a game film and making adjustments. Do the same in your profession and see how much more often you win.

Strategy I will use today: _____

_____

SEPTEMBER 13

Questions lead you to the sale and they also can lead you to resolving conflicts with customers, as well. If a customer becomes upset with you before, during or after the sale, put your mouth in neutral and your ears in overdrive. Listen and then ask questions to fully understand, which shows that you are more interested in a satisfactory resolution than you are in covering you own behind and making excuses in an attempt to defend what happened or was said. You can't win an argument and make the sale, so be prepared to take a temporary retreat during the battle so you can still win the war.

Action I will take today: _____

_____

SEPTEMBER 14

Can you recognize every objection? Are you sure? Many times customer's objections aren't as cut and dried as, "I want to think it over," or, "Your price is too high." They send you other signals and if you don't pick them up you may lose the sale. Signals as subtle as failing to make eye contact, shrugging, edging away from you, going out of their way to let everything appear to be fine as they head to the door and promise to call you back, a sudden hesitancy to communicate between couples and certain facial expressions can all be shouting out at you to pry and clarify what the real problem is. Look for these signs and ask questions to surface the objection: "If there was one thing holding you back from moving forward with this, what would it be?" or "Of what we've covered, what would you like a more in-depth explanation of?" or "Now I'm ready for all of your toughest and most pointed questions–fire away!" Your pretending like everything is okay won't get the deal done. If they're not moving forward, read between the lines and find out why before it's too late.

Today I will: _____

_____

September 15

After the real objection has surfaced, follow these steps. Isolate it to be sure that it is the only remaining objection. Ask questions to be certain that you fully understand what the problem is or if it is really a problem at all. Empathize with the customer and overcome the objection by using whatever technique is appropriate for your scenario. It may be relating a similar situation that another one of your customers found themselves in and how they handled it. It may be reducing the cost difference to the ridiculous to show them that they can't afford *not* to move forward. It may be helping them to weigh all the pros and cons in order to balance out and diminish the "cons" by putting them in the proper perspective. As you are overcoming the objection, go back and reaffirm minor points you both agree on. This keeps the momentum moving and the atmosphere productive. A strong objection is a good buying sign if you employ the right methods for isolating it and then closing on it.

Strategy I will use today: _____

September
Mid-Month Action Plan

_____

_____

_____

_____

_____

_____

_____

_____

SEPTEMBER 16

What are you afraid of? A certain type of customer? An objection? A competitor? Closing situation? Fear is natural in sales and can be used to our advantage. First of all, if you fear different types of situations, closes, objections or customers, go to work to better prepare yourself for these things. Don't let them continue to come up without having rehearsed a better plan for dealing with them. As your skills and confidence rises, your fears will diminish. Most fear results from ignorance. We fear what we don't know, or in sales, what we don't know how to handle. Preparation is the best antidote for fear. Mark Twain once said that courage was the resistance to fear, the mastery of fear, not the absence of it. It will always be there. Prepare yourself to get better at handling it. Which objection and which type of customer do you do most poorly with? Go to work to prepare yourself for the next encounter with each so you can master them.

Action I will take today: _____

_____

SEPTEMBER 17

Get visible. Do people know you are in business? Do they know who you are, what you do and where you work? Don't keep it a secret! Meet at least five new people every day. Stay in touch with your sold customers on a regular basis. Stay in touch with those you are now working on a consistent basis–even if they end up buying from someone else. Get involved with civic groups, clubs, associations, mingle at social events with people you do **not** already know. Target mail your own newsletters to groups of prospective clients and do it regularly for the name recognition. Every time you have a chance to send someone a thank you note or a note of congratulations–for anything–do it! Drop your business card in any local mail you send. Getting more visible is all about networking and marketing your presence. Getting visible is all about making something happen and not sitting back hoping it does. Are you visible enough? What can you do to put more visibility for yourself in motion?

Today I will: _____

_____

September 18

Get on the same side. Today, make a special effort to get on the same side as your prospect. Too many salespeople adopt an almost adversarial approach to selling. They have one purpose and they feel their prospect has another. These separate agendas can turn into a battleground. Establish common ground, spend plenty of time assessing their needs (this means keeping quiet and listening more!), show them what your product has in common with meeting their needs and why it's the best choice available. Then wrap it up by making it make more sense for them to go ahead with the purchase then it does for them to maintain the status quo. You'll get further faster if you get them running toward the same goal on the same path.

Strategy I will use today: _____

_____

September 19

Don't drop out of school. Don't get so wrapped up in your day-to-day hustle and bustle that you stop learning. You can be too busy to read and wind up being perceived by your customers as being too uninformed to sell your product convincingly. You can go from being too busy to listen to a motivational tape or read a motivational book to being too negative to keep around the productive people in the organization and in too much of a rut to keep around the company overall. If you think you can climb above the crowd in sales and in life without the knowledge and positive influences that continuing education brings, you have a *very slight* chance of being right. But even if you manage to get above the crowd you'll fall back down like a stone without continuing to work on yourself. It's your choice and it's a daily one.

Action I will take today: _____

_____

September 20

Be a *consultant*. "Salespeople" tend to talk too much. They pitch their product, with little regard for building rapport or discovering customer's needs. The mental image you create of yourself consulting will force you to ask more questions, learn and communicate more about your product and work **with** the customer rather than **on** customer. This shift in mindset will lead you to do more of the right things during the sales process.

Today I will: _____

_____

SEPTEMBER 21

Don't rely on telepathy. Stay in touch with your customers. Don't do it only to try and sell them something, but to stay responsive to their needs in all respects. The only way you can stay in touch with their changing needs and concerns is to maintain the relationship. The more you know about what they are doing, the better you will be able to serve their needs. If you don't stay in touch and show concern for them after the sale, someone else who shows more interest and desire for their business is going to walk away with your account. Lack of contact between you and your clients causes a detachment that creates an indifference in maintaining loyalty to you. Don't wait for them to come to you when they need something. Don't wait until you need a sale before you contact them and don't rely on telepathy. None of that will work. Only the day-to-day follow-up with your customer base will retain it as yours. Remember that a loyal customer base is something you must continually *earn*. It's not a *royalty*.

Strategy I will use today: _____

_____

SEPTEMBER 22

Stop malpractice. If a doctor prescribed medication or operations before a lengthy examination, a series of tests or a thorough diagnosis, he would be committing malpractice. If an attorney failed to use every force at his disposal to defend a client, including gaining a thorough understanding of the client's position in order to do a more proficient job of representing him before throwing together a defense, he could be in serious trouble with the Bar. Could you be subject to disbarment from the selling profession if you were evaluated on the job you did diagnosing your client's needs before offering solutions? How are your investigations? We've talked about this before. Have you developed better investigating techniques and questions? Think of the average amount of time you spend finding a customer's needs before prescribing a solution. Even if the customer thinks they know what they want, do you slow the process down long enough to ensure matching the best product to their needs? Rethink your needs discovery and see where you can improve it.

Action I will take today: _____

_____

SEPTEMBER 23

Seek out the "because." The next time someone tells you that the price of your product is too high, realize that you don't have much chance to make the sale unless you uncover the "because." "Because" gives you something to work with. It uncovers the area(s) the prospect doesn't see adequate value in your offering and that's your cue to go to work in building up the value in that area. Close the value gap and close the sale. The next time someone tells you your price is too high, before going into an all-out assault reciting the attributes of your product, find out specifically where the "because" is and you can save time, breath and the sale.

Today I will: _____

_____

SEPTEMBER 24

Tired of getting the runaround from prospects? Get interesting. The only reason you will get the runaround from potential buyers is that you have not done a sufficient job in capturing their interest and excitement for what you are selling. Regroup, revisit the basics and relearn their business and their needs. Then take what you learn and what you missed the first time around and use a more effective approach with added impact and punch. The key to this technique is to realize when you are going nowhere and realizing that your persistence may just be stubbornness in disguise, that continuing to knock on the door won't work nearly as well as stepping back and looking for another opening.

Strategy I will use today: _____

_____

SEPTEMBER 25

Prepare to go to court. Sometimes the best words you can use in closing a deal are not your own. Compile testimonial letters from customers about your product and your service. Get their permission to use them in your presentation.

Many professionals put together an evidence manual of these letters and use them as "witnesses," much like a lawyer would when they go to court. You can tell your prospects something positive about you and your product but it won't have the impact of a third party endorsement. During your presentation you tell the customer about your product. Then you show them during the demonstration. Conclude your three–part presentation by proving what you told them with your evidence manual.

Action I will take today: _____

SEPTEMBER 26

An evidence manual is a value-building closing tool that gives you an edge over the competition. In addition to customer testimonials, have a section with positive press on your company or your product in your evidence manual. This can include awards the product has won, press clippings, Consumer Guide ratings, etc. Have a section touting your product and another section with competitive comparisons. An evidence manual doesn't have to be an overwhelming mass of propaganda. Start small and add to it over time. Keep it updated and most important of all–use it! Don't put it together just to let it sit on a shelf.

Today I will: _____

SEPTEMBER 27

Never "knock" the competition. Remember though, one of your jobs is to stop your customer from making a mistake. How to do it? Surprise! An evidence manual. The value of collecting third party comparisons (from magazines, trade journals and surveys) is that you can educate your customer without ever knocking the competition. Show them the data and let them arrive at their own conclusions. It's not enough to tell them about what the article or survey said. The impact you can have by showing them is irreplaceable. What information do you have available to begin the competitive section of your evidence manual? Where can you look for more data? Take the first step and give yourself the edge over your competition.

Strategy I will use today: _____

SEPTEMBER 28

Are you outsmarting yourself right out of sales? Too many salespeople become experts on who can and cannot afford to buy products just by looking at the way they walk, dress or look. Every time you prequalify your prospects you are killing your paycheck on the installment plan. When you do it only once you are starting a habit that's hard to break. It's a trap. You may think you know who can buy and who cannot but you don't **know**. The key is to treat everyone like a buyer until they prove beyond a shadow of a doubt otherwise. Give them the benefit of the doubt. You'll be right more often than not. Even if you are wrong, you will have at least stayed on track and avoided the shortcut mentality that cuts short sales careers. Think of the last time you prequalified a customer and looked on as they bought from someone else. Felt lousy didn't it? Learn from that and don't repeat the mistake. You can't afford it financially or mentally.

Action I will take today: _____

_____

SEPTEMBER 29

Forget the financial implications for a moment and realize that pre-qualifying is just plain bad manners. It shows no courtesy or respect for your prospects and is a reflection of your own arrogance. How did you feel the last time you felt you were prequalified when you were out trying to spend your hard earned money? Infuriating wasn't it? Here's the bottom line: Prequalifying is cocky. It's shortsighted. It's habit forming. It's inexcusable, so save any rationalization you have for doing so. Prequalifying is an affront to your customers and a betrayal of your employer who is paying you to treat everyone like a buyer, so knock it off. You need to change your mindset. It's a lot easier to sit back and pick and choose who you want to wait on or call on. It takes a lot more discipline to treat everyone like a buyer until they prove otherwise and to avoid shortcuts that appear to be the easy way. Resolve today to develop the discipline and mindset to treat everyone as a buyer–just as you'd want to be treated.

Today I will: _____

_____

SEPTEMBER 30

We've put it off long enough. Let's talk about one of a sales professional's biggest enemies: procrastination. Do you procrastinate? If so, the question is, what are you afraid of? Procrastination is not a disease, it's a symptom of something else–usually related to fear. Fear of rejection, so you don't take the first step. Fear of failure, so it's easier not to try. The first step to conquering any fear is to face it, acknowledge it. Then find out more about it. The more you know about something, the less you fear it. The next step is to take some definite action toward what you are procrastinating over. Take the task in small pieces. Starting small and moving forward creates momentum and subsequent action keeps the momentum flowing. Procrastination can keep you in a rut and prevent you from getting all you can and can keep you from becoming all you can become. What have you been putting off? A follow-up system for your sold customers? Daily training to sharpen your skills? Goal setting or planning your day? Calling on a certain client? Prospecting? Identify what is holding you back and then follow the steps outlined to overcome them. The key is to do it now! Otherwise you'd be procrastinating.

Strategy I will use today: _____

SEPTEMBER
MONTH-END ACTION PLAN

_____

_____

_____

_____

_____

OCTOBER 1

Procrastination will just plain wear you out. It's exhausting. Harvard philosopher and author William James observed, "There is nothing so fatiguing as an uncompleted task." Beginning to whittle away at procrastination frees up energy. It builds self-confidence and self-esteem. This creates more energy. What action did you take yesterday to create momentum in an area you've been procrastinating in? How did it feel? What will you do today to keep it going? Continuing to follow through is essential to establishing stronger habits of achievement. Keep moving!

Action I will take today: _____

_____

OCTOBER 2

As you've been working to overcome procrastination, have you found the causes? Is it your being poorly organized? A lack of clear goals to work toward? Time <u>mis</u>management resulting from too many distractions and a lack of overall focus? Are going to work to wait instead of going with a plan to make something happen? If you are still not coming to work with a clear written plan for the day and specific goals to guide what you do, this is part of the problem. Not having a clear focus for the day, month and rest of your career fractures your effectiveness, sends you in circles, gives you many busy days where you accomplish nothing and causes procrastination. Quite frankly, you're not sure what the next move is most of the time so you get locked into the paralysis of analysis. Lots of thought, no action. Take the first step towards getting rid of procrastination by getting back to the basics of what you know you should be doing every day. Plan your day in advance and have clear goals to guide you through achieving each and every day. If you are not doing these two things, you'll never beat procrastination. Stop now and do them. If you've already done this, re-examine the planning and goal setting to make sure they are addressing the most vital areas of what you need to do.

Today I will: _____

_____

OCTOBER 3

Paint the picture. When presenting products to your customer, talk as though they already own it. Create mental ownership. They have to own it in their head before they will own it on paper. Talk about the benefits as through they were already enjoying them. Go over the positive results they will have; peace of mind, pride of ownership and the like. Paint such a convincing picture that there is more pain in letting go of the scenario you've created than there is in parting with the cash to purchase it.

Strategy I will use today: _____

OCTOBER 4

Closing the sale is a good term for wrapping up a deal, but it creates a poor mental picture of continuing the relationship with your customer. Too many salespeople take "closing" literally. They write the order, take the money and never contact the customer again–until they want to "close" another deal. Turn closing into an opening. An opening of a new relationship through follow-up contact and concern. An opening that will lead to more closing.

Action I will take today: _____

OCTOBER 5

Momentum can be a salesperson's best friend. Once you've got it going there's not much that can slow you down. When you are at a standstill, however, the smallest obstacle can keep you immobilized. There are a number of momentum-makers and momentum-breakers that you encounter every day. The greatest causes for losing momentum are usually another person, a boss, an event or an issue. Think of momentum-breakers that you have run into lately. How can you avoid or deal more effectively with them the next time they come up? By preparing for them now, you'll be in a better position to overcome them when they next arise. Find ways to start momentum and keep it going today.

Today I will: _____

OCTOBER 6

One momentum-breaker you will run into is a critical attitude. The momentum-making counter to this is a constructive attitude. If you or the people you work with have the habit of pointing out problems without offering solutions and if complaining has become so commonplace that you don't even realize you're doing it anymore, you're a "breaker." You're crippling yourself and those around you. It actually takes more energy to be critical than constructive because negative energy wears you out and positive energy uplifts you. What areas have you been too critical in? Has it been about a policy, person or a product? How can you turn your thinking around and shift from the mediocre persona of being a fault-finder to the meteoric persona of being a good-finder? Making this shift will not only make you feel better about yourself and your job, those around you will enjoy your presence more as well. Being critical is exhausting. Being constructive energizes. Make the right choice.

Strategy I will use today: _____

OCTOBER 7

Dishonesty is the ultimate momentum-breaker. Being dishonest with co-workers, customers or superiors will come full circle and sabotage your future. Any short-term gain you get from dishonesty is wiped out ten-fold in the long run. Character is a momentum-maker. Your character will determine how you see situations and opportunities. The choices you make each day comprise your character. Have there been situations or areas lately where your character has been compromised? What can you do to set things right? Remember that character is not developed when pressure situations come along–it's revealed.

Action I will take today: _____

OCTOBER 8

Focus is a momentum-maker. A focused mind develops a focused plan and thought process. These, in turn, create results. One of the most common momentum-breakers is "shot-gunning." "Shot-gunning" is shooting at everything, hoping that something gets hit. It's a double-minded approach that goes in every direction, rarely arriving at any particular destination. Shot-gunning is an energy leak. Its scattered approach reveals a scattered mind. If you suffer from shot-gunning, the first step to shifting focus is to slow down long enough to develop clear goals and specific plans of action to reach them. This will provide the pathway and guidance to a consistent and meaningful approach that will produce results. Is shot-gunning depleting your momentum? Regroup and increase your focus in those areas today.

Today I will: _____

_____

OCTOBER 9

Self-training is a momentum-maker and you have complete control over whether it gets done or not. Going with what you know and trying to stretch your current skills the entire length of your career without actively pursuing more training and knowledge is a momentum-breaker that will sink you to the depths of mediocrity. New knowledge induces enthusiasm. Enthusiasm and knowledge combined ignites action. Action fueled by knowledge and enthusiasm produces results. What have you learned lately? What knowledge are you actively pursuing? How do you plan on turning it into action?

Strategy I will use today: _____

_____

OCTOBER 10

Thinking about what you want is a momentum-maker. Thinking about what you don't want breaks your momentum and can bring you exactly what you're thinking about. You move toward what you think about–good or bad. Since you only have so much energy to go around, why would you waste any of it on thinking about what you don't want to happen. Your mind has a way of completing a picture. So focus your energy and efforts in that area. Where has your focus been lately? Where will that lead you? Remember that focusing on what you don't want is rehearsing defeat–not a very productive or profitable way to expend your valuable and limited time and energy.

Action I will take today: _____

_____

OCTOBER 11

Indecision can break your momentum and your bank account. Action is a momentum-maker. As a sales professional you have to keep things moving. Clear plans and goals make it easier to make decisions and keep the momentum going. Lulls develop when we have a fuzzy vision or poorly defined goal. They cause indecision and that leads to lost opportunities. What makes you indecisive? Increase your knowledge in that area and it's easier to make better and quicker decisions. When it comes to making that new contact, calling that old customer, picking up the book and learning about that new product, trying out the competition's product or buying the ticket for that seminar, take action. Even a small step in the right direction will create momentum.

Today I will: _____

_____

October 12

Creativity creates momentum and stale tradition breaks it. Think of your daily routine and the selling and follow-up process you go through every day. When is the last time you changed something or at least tried something different? Locking into tradition with the "that's the way we've always done it" outlook consigns you to mediocrity. Creativity provides growth and new opportunities. It also makes things more fun and keeps the juices flowing. Creativity is a great antidote for ruts. Identify the areas in your life, work routine and selling process that have become anchored to tradition. You don't necessarily have to change them overnight–but at least look at them and see what might be missing and in need of change.

Strategy I will use today: _____

_____

October 13

"Average" is your enemy. Being average in sales starts with average thinking. Average thinking accepts average efforts. Average efforts produce average results. Average results bring you anonymity in your chosen field and reduce your future to–you guessed it–being average. You can't have great tomorrows with average efforts today. In which areas have you–perhaps without even realizing it–accepted average efforts and performance? If you're getting average output in these areas, change the input. Address these areas with vigor and commit to not settling for them any more.

Action I will take today: _____

_____

October 14

Is your best good enough? Many salespeople legitimately give a sale their best and still come up short time and time again. The reality is that whatever skill level we are currently at determines our best. It would make sense, therefore, to stop using the defense that "we did our best" and go to work on the skills needed to make our best better. If your best isn't getting the job done, see it as a wake-up call to action. Think of two situations lately where you lost the sale. Did you do your best? Take a close look at exactly what you did and determine which part of your best wasn't strong enough to make the deal. Then go to work on that area. Do this exercise often. The continuous, incremental improvements you will make over time will keep you above the crowd in your field.

Today I will: _____

_____

OCTOBER 15

Can you paint over the phone? In the absence of face-to-face contact, it's imperative to paint mental pictures and images over the telephone when speaking with your customers. Clarity and communication are paramount. Use your "paintbrush" effectively when setting appointments, and the chances of actually seeing your customer after you set the appointment soar. Here's a sample script you could use after you set the appointment to paint a mental picture. Change the words to adapt to what you sell and to your own style.

"Alright, Bob, I'm writing your name and number down on my calendar for Friday at 4:45 and I'll be sure to take myself off the sales floor a little before to get that Suburban you want to look at all cleaned up, filled up and pulled over to the side. By the way, do you prefer coffee or something cold to drink? (Customer response.) Great, I'll have a pot of fresh coffee on as well. Bob, I'm scheduled kind of tight on Friday, so if you're running a little behind please give me a call so I can make a schedule adjustment and if my previous appointment is running over, I'll give you a call so you don't get here and have to wait. In fact, what number can I reach you at that time if I need to call? (Customer response) Great! I'll plan on seeing you at 4:45."

This is called anchoring an appointment with commitment. Most salespeople stop at just setting the appointment. Professionals anchor it with commitment to improve the odds that a customer will show up as scheduled. After you paint that mental picture, if they decide not to show up, they are much more likely to call you rather than just leave you hanging. When you anchor an appointment with commitment, you anchor their conscience with guilt if they don't call when they can't make it. Use this technique with the next appointment you set today. It works.

Strategy I will use today: _____

_____

October
Mid-Month Action Plan

_____

_____

_____

_____

_____

_____

_____

October 16

Another technique you can use when on the telephone is to have the customer write something down. Whenever you say, "Betty, get a pen and paper, I've got something I want you to jot down," you are maintaining control or as the case may be, taking control of the situation. This is also a great way to get their phone number. Sales psychologists say that it's easier to get something from a customer after you've given them something. So you could continue your conversation as follows: "Betty, while you have that pen and paper out go ahead and write down my name. It's Dave Anderson. And my number again is 723-9754, extension 104. What's your best daytime number, Betty? And your best evening number? And how do you spell your last name?" Always ask for theirs right after you give them yours. The timing has to be right. And ask like you expect to get it. Too many salespeople pull out their scared and whiney voice when they ask for a name or number. Asking for daytime and evening numbers is less threatening to a customer than asking for their home phone number. Try this with your next phone call today. You'll maintain control and get the number.

Action I will take today: _____

_____

October 17

Speaking of appointments, there's a right way and wrong way to try and set them. The last thing you want is a vague appointment. Ask either/or questions to help control the appointment and give your customer a choice of when to come in: "Bob, looking at my calendar I have 2:15 or 3:45 open. Which would be best for you?" This is a lot better than, "Well, Bob, when can you come in?" By setting appointments on an odd number, like on quarter-hours, you'll also increase the chances of their coming in. Odd appointments sound more precise, more credible. Professionals in sales should sound like other professionals. A doctor or attorney would never say, "Just come in anytime Tuesday afternoon," or, "Stop in and see me sometime next week." Neither should you. Use these three techniques we've gone over the past couple of days and put them all together to take your phone skills to a new level.

Today I will: _____

_____

October 18

Compete with yourself. Too many salespeople compare themselves to one another in terms of abilities or income. While this sort of friendly competition can be healthy, don't get hung up on it. In the long run, it's no great professional achievement to be superior to the people you work with. A great professional achievement is to be superior to your previous self. Are you a better closer than you were six months ago? Do you know more about your product than you did last month? The true measure of your success and the ultimate form of consistent motivation in sales lies in continually improving yourself. Play against yourself. Evaluate the top three functions of your job. What has changed lately? Can you be specific? Is it measurable? If not, what will you do differently so that when you look back three months from now you'll have better answers?

Strategy I will use today: _____

_____

October 19

Truth is too often a casualty of the sale. Get in the habit of telling the truth. It's a lot tougher to live with the ultimate consequences of not telling it than it is to face the music as it plays. There is no such thing as an inconsequential lie. Once you compromise your character and the customer's trust, a lie is a lie is a lie. Don't try to polish it up with rationalization. Somewhere along the line you have to make a decision as to what will bring you out on top over the long term of your career–taking the "easy wrong" to bail you out temporarily, or choosing the "hard right" that keeps your image, conscience and professional esteem intact.

Action I will take today: _____

_____

OCTOBER 20

What is your script mastery level? Many salespeople have a negative attitude about scripts. But whatever you are saying to your customers right now is your script. The difference is that some scripts are worth $20,000 per year and some are worth hundreds of thousands per year. The challenge is to trade in some of your less-effective scripts for some that will bring you more success. Good scripting comes from great preparation. It's being smart enough to know that certain situations will come up with your customers and going to the trouble to be ready for them. Good scripts keep the sales process moving. They keep you in control. They bypass and overcome objections and close the sale. Evaluate your scripts. Are they as effective and powerful as you would like? Do they need updating, revision or discarding? Write down your three most commonly used scripts and look for ways to make them better. Sometimes, just the change of a word, inflection or tone make all the difference.

Today I will: _____

_____

OCTOBER 21

Script mastery doesn't just come to you in a dream one night. They are perfected with repetitious practice, drilling and rehearsing. There are no shortcuts. Just hearing them on a tape or watching them on a video isn't enough. Mastery comes with saying the words and using them over and over. This brings them to a level where they are reflexive. That's the key. You don't and can't take time to think about them. They have to become a reflex. They have to flow easily and they must sound like *conversation*. Only practice brings this level of mastery to reality. Remember, practice doesn't make perfect, perfect practice makes perfect. What do you do to master your scripts? Do you only use bits and pieces or do you "own" your most important scripts? Go to work to refine your practice system for turning scripts into viable tools.

Strategy I will use today: _____

_____

October 22

What will you change today? Is everything perfect? If not, then something must change. It doesn't have to be drastic. It does have to be at least a small step in the right direction. It doesn't have to solve a problem all by itself, but it should start positive momentum that way. Too many salespeople find reasons not to change. If everything is completely perfect, this would be understandable. Until everything is perfect however, you should look for some positive step to take each day in some area to move towards improvement and perfection. Don't worry about achieving perfection. You never will. But the journey toward it holds substantial and numerous rewards. You can't go to a higher level by holding onto lower ground. Change something today.

Action I will take today: _____

_____

October 23

Too many people don't change because they don't want to appear inconsistent. In moral and ethical areas this is more than acceptable. In your daily routine and habits however, this reasoning is hogwash. Emerson once said that foolish consistency is the hobglobin of small minds. Churchill remarked that he'd rather be right than consistent. Foolish consistency consigns you to getting what you've always been getting and missing the challenges that pass your way each day. Foolish consistency is the stuff ruts are made of. If you're not changing anything because of consistency, you're just playing it safe. And if you're playing it safe you're separating yourself from the biggest opportunities you'll ever have within your reach. Where have you been playing it safe? Think with an open mind and be honest. How can you move out of that comfort zone and get the rest of what you have coming as a professional in sales?

Today I will: _____

_____

October 24

Stop taking challenges so personally. By personalizing problems and challenges that come your way, you immobilize yourself from learning and capitalizing on them. Make up your mind that there are no bad experiences. Look for the good in each experience and be determined to learn from it. You'll stop classifying experiences as good or bad. You'll also stop wasting all the energy involved in

taking them personally. Think of something recently that you classified as bad.
Looking back, can you see where there may have been something positive to
come out of it, another door opened, a valuable lesson learned? Were you able
to teach a lesson to another? If you can't find something good in something bad
that happened, try harder. It's there. Once you find it, you can learn, go forward
and do so with absence of fear from other bad experiences. Remember that nothing has any meaning other than the meaning you give it.

Strategy I will use today: _____

_____

OCTOBER 25

Create a larger vision of what you can be today. The key word here is create. Too
many people wait for a vision to pop into their head and end up missing the boat.
See yourself as you can be in the areas of skills, finances, relationships and position. Now, think of where you really are in these areas. Hold your vision tightly
and put a plan together to make up the difference. Start the ball moving. Take action today and everyday, regardless of how small it seems. Creating your vision is
the first step, going on to fulfill it has to follow. The vision of some salespeople is
like their reflection in the mirror. They can't see anything other than what's right
in front of them. Where have your sights been deadlocked? Income? Position?
Skill level? Create your vision to see beyond that point. Oliver Wendell Holmes
said that once a mind is stretched to a new idea, it never returns to its original di-
mension. In other words, once you take the time to stretch your mind, things won't
be the same again. They'll be better. With this in mind, what are you waiting for?

Action I will take today: _____

_____

OCTOBER 26

Are you afraid that your follow-up with a customer might be perceived as too
pushy or high-pressure? Do you use this as an excuse not to do a better job of
following up? The fact is that most people appreciate professional persistence
from sales people. Persistent follow-up is an opportunity to show your customer
that you want and value their business. In reality, the lack of follow-up can be
perceived as indifference or apathy. Your customer can't help but wonder that if
you don't show an interest in them and their needs before you have the money
from the sale, what kind of service and concern can be expected after you have
the sale? Dig out those working deals where you feared you might be pushing

too hard. Call the customers and let them know that you genuinely want and need their business and that you want to address any questions or concerns that might be holding them back from going through with it and nothing bad will happen.

Today I will: _____

_____

October 27

How successful would you be in your career if you were addicted to illegal drugs? Could you accomplish all you wanted to and continue to climb to the next level? Probably not, over the long term. Being addicted to mediocrity is just as detrimental as any drug on the market. Mediocrity is an addiction. It has to be broken. It debilitates your drive, robs you of joy and causes you to sleepwalk through your career. The best rehab for mediocrity is to take a hard, honest look at where you are and ask yourself if this is the best you can do or if there is more you are capable of. Then go to work to make yourself more capable. Chances are that you can get a lot accomplished with the same skill level you are at anyway. Making yourself more capable just doubles the benefit. Think of at least two areas where you have allowed mediocrity to creep into your performance. Decide what's no longer acceptable and resolve to stretch beyond it mediocrity's grasp today!

Strategy I will use today: _____

_____

October 28

Envy will distract you and absorb your positive energy. Too many salespeople become obsessed with others in their organization who are having success. Simple admiration can be healthy and even motivating, but severe envy can become disastrous. It can cause you to lose your focus, change your selling style and cripple your productivity. Get to know the top producers who are getting your attention. Reduce the distance between you and them. You'll find that they have problems and challenges just like you do. Take them off the pedestal you've put them on and get back to minding your own business and developing your own skills without worrying about someone else's. You cannot effectively do both.

Action I will take today: _____

_____

OCTOBER 29

When it comes to prescribing solutions, timing is everything. It's tempting to jump right in when talking to a client and throw out a solution you feel sure will work for them. However, even if it is a good solution, if the customer feels they haven't had a chance to express their needs completely your solution will lose its impact. Hear your customers out. Ask lots of questions. Resist the urge to offer too quick a solution to what may be a major problem or purchase in their life. Jumping the gun can make you appear insensitive to the importance of their situation or disinterested in finding out more about it.

Today I will: _____

_____

OCTOBER 30

Watch out for mixed signals from customers. Customers emit buying signals verbally, through tone and inflection, and with their body language. When the verbiage they use conflicts with the body language they are sending out, believe the body language and act on it accordingly. Read a book on body language. (*How To Read A Person Like A Book* by Gerard Nierenberg is excellent.) It can be a key to good timing. For instance, you would never want to ask a closing question while a customer had his arms crossed in front of him. Nor would you want to ask while he was in a laid back position with hands behind his head. You need to get the arms unfolded and the customer interested enough to be leaning in before you ask the question. You should also become more aware of the body language signals you are giving out. You can give yourself away just as easily as you can read a customer. Body language is a two-way street. Get both ways working for you.

Strategy I will use today:_____

_____

OCTOBER 31

Get powerful! Use power phrases when closing a sale with a customer. Phrases like you've earned it, you've worked hard, you deserve it, will open new doors for you and it'll make you feel like a million bucks. Your customer generally won't argue with words like these. They put pizzazz in your close and help your client reach back for that last little bit of justification they may need to feel right about the purchase. Use power phrases to power your sales to the next level. Remember, sales aren't missed by a few dollars, they're missed by a few words.

Action I will take today: _____

OCTOBER
MONTH-END ACTION PLAN

_____

_____

_____

_____

_____

_____

_____

_____

_____

_____

_____

_____

NOVEMBER 1

Take time over money. Time is more valuable. You can always get more money. You cannot get more time. Use your time wisely. Guard it jealously. Learn to make use of your down time. The time you have to spend waiting for a client or for a meeting to begin. Form the habit of carrying important files around with you to go through during these times. Carry an "A" file of important projects or reading material. Ten minutes here and ten minutes there starts to really add up over the course of your month. Don't become neurotic and feel like you've got to be doing something every single minute of the day. In fact, if you'll use your down time at work efficiently, you'll find more time left over after work to enjoy the rest of your life's activities.

Action I will take today: _____

_____

NOVEMBER 2

Do you work in an action environment? To save time, you should have a place for everything, whether at your office or working on the road. Taking time to organize and have your most essential tools readily accessible saves time and frustration. It will also keep your work flowing with momentum. Interruptions to go find paperwork, staples or legal pads break productive work patterns and throw you off track. Keep an action environment working for you. On the road, make it a mobile action environment by taking the time in advance to stock what you need. If you are serious about saving time and getting the most out of each minute in a day, invest the effort to be prepared in advance. What is your action environment missing that you should get now?

Today I will: _____

_____

NOVEMBER 3

Make more calls than you take. Time management experts estimate that it takes twelve minutes to handle a typical incoming call and only seven minutes to complete one that you planned and initiated. Take this five minute difference and multiply it by a dozen or so calls per day and you're up to an hour of saved time. Incoming calls tend to turn into rambling sessions. You can't afford the wasted time. Be proactive and initiate as many calls as you can. This means getting right on top of customer "heat" cases and resolving them before they turn into bigger time leaks. Saving five minutes here and another five minutes there adds up to real time–and money–over the course of your month.

Strategy I will use today: _____

_____

NOVEMBER 4

To minimize your time spent on projects, form the habit of handling the paperwork for any project only once. Either do it, ditch it or delegate it. Don't keep shuffling it and moving it from "in" box to "out" box and back. Keep moving. Handling the same work over and over again is a momentum-breaker. Form the discipline to do it, ditch it or delegate it and you'll be buying time to focus on the next sale and avoid the costly habit of rehashing yesterday's news.

Action I will take today: _____

_____

NOVEMBER 5

Become a finisher. Focus on and finish projects before moving on to other projects. Have a plan for each project, break it down into little steps and keep moving toward its completion. Once you establish a record of finishing for yourself, it's easier to finish the next project and then the next. You'll gain momentum. Keep a list of finished projects for self-motivation. Remind yourself of victories and you'll want to keep adding to the list.

Today I will: _____

_____

NOVEMBER 6

Enlarge your goals. This is a great intellectual exercise to generate ideas. For instance, if you normally sell $30,000 worth of product in a month, enlarge the goal to $60,000 and start generating the ideas you'll need to get there. The object is not for this to actually become your goal, but by acting as though it were, you will force yourself to think at a different level. You'll come up with tactics that will put you far past whatever your ordinary goal was because you'll be thinking in terms of and moving toward twice that number. Do this the next time you set a forecast or goal for yourself and watch the new power and raised sights you'll develop.

Strategy I will use today: _____

_____

NOVEMBER 7

Act. The best way to become motivated is to take action. Too many salespeople wait until they feel like acting. What if the feeling never comes? Nothing gets done! The key is to act your way into feeling motivated. Start acting on and doing what you need to get done and the motivation will follow. You motivate yourself by turning thinking into action, not by waiting for thinking to make you feel like acting. Just do it!

Action I will take today: _____

_____

NOVEMBER 8

Are you fairly happy and comfortable with where you are today? Many salespeople are. They are making more money and having more success than in any other job in their lives. Their income is comfortable and so are they. The problem is that what makes you comfortable today is not necessarily going to be what you need to be comfortable in the future (skills, income, customer base, etc.). It's easy to get lulled into comfort today and not put anything into motion to bring forth the positive changes you will need down the road. When it becomes obvious (in the future) that you need to change, it's often too late. You cannot become what you want to become and need to become by remaining as you are. Look for areas where you are comfortable. Will you still be comfortable at these levels in the future? If not, start improving your position today. Don't wait until it's too late.

Today I will: _____

_____

NOVEMBER 9

Change is an uncomfortable topic for salespeople. It's not so much that there is resistance to change. Instead, it's more a matter of resisting being changed. It's like the old joke about how many salespeople it takes to change a light bulb. Four. One to change it and the other three to reminisce about how great the old bulb was. There is always internal and external pressure to change. Peer pressure can cripple your efforts to improve your skills, habits and attitudes. Einstein once said, "Great spirits will always encounter violent opposition from mediocre people." Take a look at the areas you identified with yesterday as being too comfortable. Take the most important item on that list and commit to beginning to change it today. Reflect on your progress at mid-day and again at the end of the day. Do this for six weeks and then move onto the next item. Stay in productive and consistent motion. It's hard to get stuck in a rut when you are flying upward. It's when you stand in one place too long and begin to sink that a rut develops.

Strategy I will use today: _____ _____

_____

N OVEMBER 10

Take it easy. When you first approach a prospect and have gone through your initial greeting, try talking about anything other than something related to the sale. Put the prospect at ease. Jumping in too soon, before your prospect is ready to listen and accept what you are saying can make them very uncomfortable and even defensive. Practice small talk. Don't ramble on for too long, talk just enough to break the ice and open them up to you as a person. Remember, if you seem tense and in a hurry, they will pick up on it and draw into a shell. If you are relaxed and friendly, this will set the tone as well.

Action I will take today: _____

_____

N OVEMBER 11

Not so fast. When encountering an objection from a customer avoid quick, snappy answers. A reply that's too speedy can backfire and give the buyer the impression that you are a know-it-all or are confrontational. It also may send the signal that you are not listening closely enough to their concern. Firing back a reply may not give the prospect the feeling that their concern is being fairly considered or understood. Besides, you may be 100% right in your reply, but if the customer doesn't appreciate your style, what you are will speak so loudly that they won't hear what you are saying. How you reply is just as important as what you say. Practice slowing down your replies today. Increase the space of time before their response and your reply. Speak slowly and thoughtfully when you do respond. The customer will be more ready to listen at this point.

Today I will: _____

_____

November 12

Practice not choking. Some salespeople get so intense and wrapped up in the process of making the sale that they forget to focus on the customer. They are too focused on the sale. The goal, of course, is to focus on the customer. Make them feel so at ease and confident in you and the product that wrapping up the sale will seem like a "rubber stamp." Practice showing your customer you are more interested in them than in the sale and you'll get the sale.

Strategy I will use today: _____

_____

November 13

Want to change your thinking and attitude about everyone you meet, whether they buy or not? Start viewing everyone as a customer. They won't all buy when you want them to, but with the right outlook and good follow-up they can all become your customers. Adapting this outlook will give you a longer term perspective on building relationships with your customers and no customer will ever again seem like a waste of time. Change your thinking and you'll change your long-term customer base, which will in turn change your sales and income. Start treating everyone you meet today like a customer. Then go to work to see that they become one.

Action I will take today: _____

_____

November 14

Never, never, never tell your customers that they don't understand something. **Never** argue with them. **Never** tell them they are wrong. First of all, when it appears your customer doesn't understand, you take the blame and apologize for not being thorough enough and then go back through the explanation. Secondly, when your customer disagrees with you, agree to disagree. Hear them out, show empathy for their position and explain yours. Finally, point out areas where you do agree and have common ground. Then show that you understand their point of view in the areas you disagree with, following with a more defined explanation of your viewpoint. The goal is to paint a compelling enough case for the client to see that your point has validity, without them having to admit they are wrong or walking away from a deal due to pride.

Today I will: _____

_____

NOVEMBER 15

Don't knock your competition. Doing so cheapens your presence as a professional and detracts from building value in what *you* are selling. Knocking a competitor is easy. It's a lot tougher to learn enough about their product to show your prospect why what you are offering will better fill their needs. There is also a chance that your prospect has done business with the competitor before, or knows someone who works there. Who is your biggest competitor? Identify them and go to work to learn everything you can about them. Then become an expert at communicating the benefits of buying from you, your company and your product. This is salesmanship. The alternative is cheap slander. Even if what you say is true, your customer's perception is what carries weight–and most will perceive self-serving slander.

Strategy I will use today: _____

NOVEMBER
MID-MONTH ACTION PLAN

_____

_____

_____

_____

_____

_____

_____

NOVEMBER 16

Try the following approach when your prospect tells you that they have a better product or a better price from a competitor: "Mr. Customer, let me share a few reasons with you that will explain why so many customers just like you are choosing our product over Brand X." Then go into a value-building presentation that edifies your product or service without throwing mud on the competition. Or, in a case where a prospect is looking at the same brand in your store and comparing it with an identical, yet cheaper brand in another store, try this, "Mr. Customer, let me share a few reasons with you that will explain why purchasing this product from us is your best investment." Then sell the value and advantages of your company, your service and you. Be prepared and you can turn their objections and comparisons into closing situations for yourself.

Action I will take today: _____

_____

NOVEMBER 17

What happens to you during the day is only ten percent of the equation. The other ninety percent rests in how you respond. This is an important principle to grasp. During the typical sales day there are numerous opportunities to react wrongly to what happens; for instance, you may encounter an angry customer, you lose a sale, an unpleasant encounter with a supervisor. Your strength lies in the ability to choose your response. You may not be able to control what happens, but you can control what you do about it. Take advantage of this power and stop letting minor issues become major stumbling blocks. What do you tend to react to? Think and plan on how you can respond more constructively the next time it comes up. Be prepared in advance and you'll be amazed at the difference an outlook and attitude can have on how well you can handle the same things that used to cause so much grief in the past.

Today I will: _____

_____

NOVEMBER 18

Do you "flock?" Too many salespeople go to work to fit in and be liked, not to make a lucrative living. This is not to knock cooperation and teamwork, as both are vital components to a successful company and your successful career. Just know where to draw the line. Visiting, gossiping and other small talk causes you irreparable harm. It costs time and money. Go to work to work. Stay focused. This may generate peer pressure because when you get serious and decide to turn pro in sales, it'll push the people you work with out of their own comfort zone. Remember, eagles don't flock. You find them one at a time.

Strategy I will use today: _____

_____

NOVEMBER 19

There is always a price to get to the next level in selling. Skills to develop, goals to set, disciplines to acquire and habits to build. The alternative to paying the necessary price is to consign yourself to an average career rooted in mediocrity. The best policy is to pay now and play later. You can, if you choose, play now and pay later. Just be warned that the longer in your career you wait to pay the price for the necessary skills, habits, and attitudes to climb to new levels, the higher the price. What price have you been paying in these areas? Have you been coasting more than you like to admit? You can keep on coasting if you like, but when the wake-up call comes to get serious about making more money and having more success, the price tag to pay will have compounded several times over. Pay now and you can play later. There are no shortcuts.

Action I will take today: _____

_____

NOVEMBER 20

Check your mental disposition. One of the classic signs of an underachiever is to blame others for their hardships and lack of success. This is a misdirected waste of energy and resources. Rarely does any one person ever stand in our way as we climb up the ladder of success to prevent us from getting there. We usually manage to keep tripping ourselves up on the way there. In fact, if we could just get out of our own way, there'd be no limit to how high we could go. If you could kick the person most responsible for your problems, you wouldn't be able to sit down for weeks! Identify key areas where you have been getting in your own way–not planning, no follow-up, not knowing enough about the product or your competitors or having a negative attitude, and go to work to remove these areas from your path. You cause yourself more woe than any outside circumstance. The good news is that you can also remedy that situation. You have control. Accept it and start getting out of your own way.

Today I will: _____

_____

November 21

There are three main levels of sales results that you can fit into. In identifying where you fall, it's easier to put a plan together to get to the next level. The three areas are survival, success and true significance. Where are you? Too many people get to the successful stage and settle for it. They lose some of the drive they had when they were just surviving. They compare themselves to others who are just surviving and this brings forth a feeling of being better than the norm. What a shame to settle for this. You cheat yourself and your company. What would it take for you to reach true significance in sales? Identify what that means to you. Define the rewards of getting there. Put a plan together to make up the difference between where you are and where true significance is. Feel that small spark start to ignite? Feels good, doesn't it? That small spark can turn into a raging inferno if you'll just follow through and let it. Go for it, starting today.

Strategy I will use today: _____

_____

November 22

Are you finding gold or filth? You'll find what you expect to find. If you start each day looking for the gold, you're likely to find it. If you are looking for the downside, the negatives, you will find them as well. What are your expectations of today? Is it going to be just another day or can it be the best day you've ever had in your career? You get to choose your approach–today and every day. Choose carefully. You just might get what you are expecting.

Action I will take today: _____

_____

November 23

Are you here today? Are you really here in mind and body? Salespeople sell out the present because they are still either hung up on the past or too focused on the future. We should look at the past–but only long enough to learn from it, make course corrections and go on. We should also look to the future. But the most productive way to do this is to have goals set with plans that have to be implemented today. "Open the present." Don't live in the past unless you like guilt and don't live in the future unless you like fear. Make today count. Milk if for all it's worth. You can't change the past but by "opening the present" you can predict the future–by creating it.

Today I will: _____

_____

November 24

How many private victories did you have yesterday? How many do you plan to have today? Private victories are the self-disciplines you need to sharpen your skills, habits attitudes and overall performance. They can consist of anything from learning more about your product, taking better care of your health, reading or listening to inspiring and motivational material and practicing a presentation or script for closing. The number of public victories you have (most notably, sales and income) will be in direct proportion to the private victories that precede them. If you've been going only for public victories without paying attention to the private ones, the public wins become fewer and farther between. Plan a week full of private victories, then work on them for a month. Add to them and refine them wherever necessary until they become a habit and part of your life.

Strategy I will use today: _____

_____

November 25

Are you more interested in beating the other salespeople in your organization or in bettering yourself? There is a huge difference. Some salespeople get so caught up in trying to beat the next guy, their own self-improvement is subordinated and diminished to the point to where it doesn't matter–just as long as they finish first today. When you are spending too much time watching everyone else, your focus is diluted. Half of your attention is on the other guy and only the remaining half is devoted to yourself. Concentrate totally on what you can do to best yourself. How can you get better? Work on the areas that you can control and stop wasting valuable and irreplaceable energy fretting over things that you cannot. As you make yourself better, you will get more than your share of the winning that takes place within your organization.

Action I will take today: _____

NOVEMBER 26

Learn to say no. Your time is valuable and irreplaceable. It is more valuable than money–you can get more money but not more time. Protect your time by learning to say no to opportunities to overextend yourself or immerse yourself in trivial activities that don't fit into your goals and plans for professional success. Each time you say yes to something that's not important, you say no to something that is. Once you have clear goals, a strong mission and set of priorities, saying no becomes much easier. You simply hold the potential time-waster up to the light of your goals and mission and if it doesn't fit, say no and go on. You won't lose your focus and you won't waste your time.

Today I will: _____

NOVEMBER 27

Stop taking fish and start learning how to fish. Surely, you've heard the saying, "Give a man a fish and you feed him for a day, teach him to fish and you feed him for a lifetime?" The question is, are you taking fish or learning to fish? Taking fish can amount to selling the "give-me" accounts and customers that are going to be with you, regardless of conditions. These would also include freebie deals flipped to you from supervisors, house deals and the like. They would also encompass deals which you started but didn't have the skills to complete, so someone else comes in and closes the deal for you. Start learning how to fish–developing the skills necessary to create and close your own deals and to build your own business. This is the only long-term security in sales. Relying on "laydowns" or the law of averages to put some deals on the board is the path of least skill, least resistance, least job security, least job satisfaction and least paycheck. In what areas have you been taking "fish," and where could you start doing some "fishing?"

Strategy I will use today: _____

Selling Above The Crowd

November 28

How's your timing been lately? It is true that buyers love to be asked for the order, in fact they expect it. However, this is only true when it occurs at the right time, after rapport is established, needs determined, value built and concerns addressed. Some people feel like they have a problem closing the deal–but the problem may not have anything to do with their closes. If your closing has been tougher than usual lately, take a look at the timing. Your closes may be just fine.

Action I will take today: _____

_____

November 29

Know when to quit. Any good negotiation should be a win/win for the buyer and seller. No one builds much of a customer base going for win/lose with a customer and few businesses will exist for long by accepting lose/win with their customers. When a negotiation cannot turn into a win/win for you and the customer, go for one last alternative; no deal. Being able to walk away from a deal where someone will have to lose is the most professional and mature thing a savvy sales person can do. Try it next time. When you call "no deal" and get together again later for another try with a fresh approach, get ready to watch a win/win take place. Why? Because you and the other party will know by that time that it's the only way you'll be able to do business together.

Today I will: _____

_____

November 30

Confidence sells. Clumsiness kills. Your prospects can very often "smell blood." They know when you are prepared. They know when you're winging it. They can tell when you care about them or when you just need the numbers. A perceived lack of confidence and preparation will bring forth more objections and a slower buying cycle. On the other hand, proper preparation builds confidence and nips many objections and concerns in the bud before they ever have a chance to manifest. You cannot shortcut preparation and be effective, and you can't fake it for long. You'll be found out and unmasked for all to see. Prepare. Practice. Learn about your prospect and your product. Develop skills so you can apply them. Anything else is reducing yourself to being an order-taker hoping to get lucky.

Strategy I will use today: _____

_____

November
Month-End Action Plan

_____

_____

_____

_____

_____

_____

_____

_____

_____

_____

_____

_____

December 1

Do you take the money and run? If so, you won't be doing it for long. Too many salespeople feel that after the sale is closed it's time to go out looking for new "blood." While this is partially valid, the other half of the equation is what makes or breaks you over the course of your career. That half of the equation is contacting and maintaining a relationship with your customer after they have the product and you have the money. How easy it is for us to forget, and oh, the regret we reap down the road. Many salespeople haven't followed up with customers for years and have resigned themselves to a lack of repeat and referral business that could cut their working hours in half and double their income. It's never too late to start a follow-up program. A combination of mail and phone calls is most effective. Set up a timetable that works best for you. There is not one best system. There is a worse system; doing nothing.

Action I will take today: _____

_____

December 2

Don't be a know-it-all. A know-it-all is anyone who has stopped seeking out new information in their field. Salespeople usually become know-it-alls without even realizing it. They don't set out to become one, it just happens. There may be some areas where you have continued to learn and grow, but others where you have stopped. Think for a moment about the numerous areas involved in your job. In which areas have you become a know-it-all? How can you kick-start your momentum and begin growing in these areas again? The antidote is simple. Start learning again. Remember, learning is a process that should never stop. Seek out knowledge and apply it in all vital areas. Know-it-alls never make it above the crowd in sales success for long. Take a look around where you work. How many know-it-alls do you see? Rise above their ranks today.

Today I will: _____

_____

December 3

Don't be a wheelbarrel. Wheelbarrels in sales are those who are totally useless unless someone else fills them up, points them in the right direction and pushes them to where they need to go. It's not your manager's job to get you to the next level. Fill yourself with knowledge, a positive outlook and the desire to be the best. Point yourself in the right direction with goals, plans and an unshakable focus on being better than you were yesterday. Push yourself to the next level. Do the right things every day–even when you don't feel like it. Push hard, push often and keep pushing. Take responsibility for yourself. You can't coast above the crowd–you have to climb there.

Strategy I will use today: _____

_____

DECEMBER 4

Baloney! There is a story of two workers sitting down for lunch when one of them looks inside of his sandwich and exclaims, "Baloney again! I hate baloney! This is the third time this week I've had to eat it! This is really getting old!" The other worker looks over at him and asks, "Why don't you tell your wife not to put baloney in your lunch?" The distraught friend replied, "My wife doesn't make my lunch, I do." The moral of this story is that you put most of your own baloney in your life. What baloney have you been feeding yourself lately about your abilities, limitations or aspirations? Get out of your own way and ditch the excuses. Write them down on a piece of paper and then, in big letters, write "Baloney" next to them. Then start to focus on the real solution to these areas–the ones you can control.

Action I will take today: _____

_____

DECEMBER 5

Find feedback. Too often we feel threatened by feedback because we feel it hurts our self-esteem and we let it shake our confidence. The truth is that feedback, from the right sources, can be the best way for you to grow. You must have an open mind and a real desire to improve. Drop your defenses and listen to what is being said–not with the goal of preparing an adequate response, but listen with the goal of learning and improving what you do. Which areas stand out as areas where some feedback could help you grow? Is it in your daily habits and routine? Could it be in your efforts–or lack of efforts–to learn new techniques and increase your product knowledge? Is there some feedback that could help you better build rapport with the customers you deal with? Don't let feedback threaten you. Let it uncover your blind spots so you can correct them. Use it as a tool to grow and aid you in your climb above the crowd. Set yourself above the crowd by actually seeking out feedback–not hoping you don't hear it.

Today I will: _____

_____

December 6

Time's up! Remember that on any encounter–in phone or in person–that you have less than 30 seconds to make a favorable first impression and generate an interest in dealing with you. You will succeed in doing this when you have a well-prepared opening statement, a friendly tone and manner, and enthusiasm that separates you from the normal mass of hum-drum salespeople filling the ranks today. Never underestimate the impact of those first few seconds. Too often we are in such a hurry to get on to the business of business that we shortcut this vital step and we never get a second chance to do it right again. Remember, the most important step to the sale is the one you are on and that begins with your opening. Build momentum and set the tone with the right first impression.

Strategy I will use today: _____

_____

December 7

Don't overlook the "old-fashioned." Taking the time to establish common ground may seem old-fashioned and slow-paced in today's breakneck sales environment. The problem is that there is no substitute for its power to lead to the sale. Common ground helps your prospect identify with you and sets you apart from competitors. Common ground forgives many sins. It can overcome disadvantages you have in quality and price and can stave off rivals trying to displace you. Establishing common ground is an investment in time and energy. As old-fashioned as it may seem, take the time to find your prospect's heart before you ask them for their hand. Focus on spending extra time today establishing common ground with your customers. See how much easier it makes the rest of the sales process.

Action I will take today: _____

_____

December 8

Sincerely compliment your prospect. Take the opportunity to affirm their knowledge, track record, abilities and reputation. Affirm them and you create a climate conducive to mutual respect and trust that you'll need to begin and maintain a solid business relationship. When you realize how few compliments most people ever get, you can understand the positive and irreplaceable impact you can have by putting forth sincere compliments in a positive and professional manner. Go out of your way to look for reasons to compliment today. It's a positively addictive and productive behavior.

Today I will: _____

_____

December 9

Take it one step at a time. Too many salespeople blow cold prospecting calls because they try to go too far too fast. Keep the big picture in mind and try making your conquest in steps rather than in one, giant, impatient leap. Use your first call to a customer as an introductory call. Establish who you are, what you do and where you work. Use the first call as a device to build rapport and generate an interest. Your prospect will be relieved at your approach and much more willing to see you the next time you call. Remember, successful prospecting and cold-calling does not mean you go out strictly to seek and sell to strangers. Instead, it begins with letting people know who you are, what you do and where you work. Lay the groundwork for the next call. This approach will work if you have the patience to work it.

Strategy I will use today: _____

_____

December 10

Prospecting and cold calling in the manner discussed yesterday takes the fear out of the process–for you and the prospect. The fear is taken out for you because you won't face the rejection you face when going out on a call and heading right for the throat. The fear is also removed for the customer who now sees you as a professional interested in his needs and a solid relationship and not just a "quick-kill." You can use this approach–just letting people know who you are, what you do and where you work–to network and self-promote everywhere you go. Just get good at being low key about it and you'll be surprised at the leads that appear just by simply spreading your own word. Step out of your comfort zone and try this approach at the next couple of stops you make to buy something. Rather than just handing your money over to the grocer, waiter, doctor, accountant, gas station attendant or store clerk, *network* yourself while you're there.

See how quickly this proactive approach builds your customer base. It sure beats sitting around and waiting for something to happen.

Action I will take today: _____

_____

DECEMBER 11

Take more of an interest in your customer's success. In fact, act as though your own success depended on their success. It just might! Too many salespeople give the impression that all is well as long as they are making their sale and taking home their commission. They never show any interest or concern about the customer's business overall. No inquiries are ever made on how they can be of further help to boost the client's business or network. This selfish outlook thwarts your potential. Dynamic relationships are built with clients when you show interest and concern for their welfare and their business; and not just as it pertains to getting your order. Which of your customers can you begin creating a more meaningful relationship with by aligning your concerns with theirs? Over time, this builds a formidable and often inseparable alliance with your customer base. When they feel they have your genuine concern and friendship–your heart, as well as your service and hard work at their disposal–it becomes almost impossible to sell you out to any competitor who comes along with his hand out but heart absent.

Today I will: _____

_____

DECEMBER 12

Remember birthdays and anniversaries. To further endear yourself to the customers who help you make your living, remember their special days. Develop a logging and tracking system that allows you to send cards on birthdays, anniversaries, etc. Most people have close friends and some relatives that they never hear from on these days. Think of the impression you'll make when they hear from you. It won't be forgotten–ever. Take the time necessary today to begin to put this system in place. Get organized and make it happen. It's one competitive edge no one can ever take away from you.

Strategy I will use today: _____

_____

DECEMBER 13

Come bearing gifts. Don't be predictable. Have an ample supply of quotes, pertinent anecdotes and trade clippings that set you apart from every other sales associate and create excitement and a genuine welcome whenever you show up. You don't need anything big or glitzy. Small and meaningful will do just fine. The other salespeople your prospects deal with are so mundane and repetitious that it doesn't take much to stand out from them and make an impact. Keep your eyes open for materials you can use for motivational materials, ideas for meetings, promotions, trade news–you get the idea. What type of gift arsenal can you begin to put together for your customers? Take a look around and use your imagination. The paybacks are unbelievable and the process is lots of fun.

Action I will take today: _____

_____

DECEMBER 14

Apologize, admit and seek. How you handle complaints and problems that your prospects and customers have determines how long you stay on top with their business. When there has been a mistake or a problem arises, apologize, regardless of fault. You can't win an argument and keep a customer–not for very long anyway. Apologizing takes the sting out of any situation. Then, admit that there should be a resolution, even if you don't know what it will be. Seek that solution in good faith and as quickly as possible. When you screw up, give your customers a chance to express their feelings. Don't try to bury them under a barrage of promises. Unexpressed feelings never die. They are buried alive and just rear their head at a later date, bigger and uglier than ever before. The key to this three-step process is knowing up front what you will do when the situation arises. The situation *will* arise. When it does, knowing in advance that you will apologize, admit and seek will turn the situation around in your favor immediately. Handling difficult situations is easy when you have decided and committed in advance to what you will do. Make that commitment now.

Today I will: _____

_____

DECEMBER 15

Try this the next time you are negotiating with a customer over the price of your product: Ask them what they are willing to give up in order to get to the price they desire. Naturally, no one wants to give up anything. The point is that by asking this question you rebuild credibility in your price. Too often, our first reaction is to drop the price. Once you start this there will be no end in sight and many times you can never make the price "cheap" enough to please your customer. If you do drop the price, always remove part of the value of what they are getting. Otherwise you are sending the signal that your price was too high. Besides, negotiation is supposed to be a two-way street; give and take. Too often we are so busy giving we forget to make the customer do their part.

Strategy I will use today: _____

_____

DECEMBER
MID-MONTH ACTION PLAN

_____

_____

_____

_____

_____

DECEMBER 16

When negotiating using yesterday's scenario, you may still run into resistance from a customer who doesn't want to give anything up and is calling your bluff to drop your price. Try this next tactic to restore even more credibility to what you are asking, "Mr. Customer, since we can't come to terms on what you are willing to pay, I'll take your name and number down and if we ever run our product on sale for the price you are asking, I'll give you a call." This "take-away" close usually gets your point across, that you are at the bottom of where you can go and if they are serious about the purchase, they'll normally step up and make the deal. You can't blame the customer for trying to get the best deal. What's important is that you communicate very clearly where that point is in a convincing, professional manner.

Action I will take today: _____

_____

DECEMBER 17

Often overlooked in negotiating is asking the customer where they are coming up with the price they are offering. How did they arrive at that figure? Are they comparing our product to something else? Do they not see the value? Specifically, why are they insisting on the figure they are offering? Once you determine this you can better address what the real objection is and can develop a strategy on how to handle it. Stop trying to overcome an objection without clarifying why it exists. Start asking where their offer came from.

Today I will: _____

_____

DECEMBER 18

Shift the focus. When encountering objections, don't invest your time defending yourself and your product. Instead, restate the customer's problems and needs. Focus on them and reposition your solutions to meet those needs and solve those problems. Too often we lose sight of our objective–meeting a customer's needs and solving their problems. When we get caught up in being defensive, we often never regain control. When negotiating, keep the main thing the main thing. And the main thing is solving your customer's problems and meeting needs. Both parties should remain aware of this at all times. It leads to win/win solutions.

Strategy I will use today: _____

_____

DECEMBER 19

Add one step. Take a look at your goals. Even if you've been setting and evaluating them regularly and writing out a plan and a time line, there is probably one step missing that would make you more effective. *Who's holding you accountable?* Knowing that you'll be held accountable for your progress tends to keep you focused. Pick a partner–it could be a family member, friend or spouse–and decide to get together once a week to talk about how you've done. Remember that everything you do to increase your adherence and commitment to what you do will put you and keep you above the crowd more solidly.

Action I will take today: _____

_____

DECEMBER 20

Avoid "Toxic People." In the opening chapters of this book we talked about the importance of attitude and keeping away from the "grave-diggers." These people are toxic. It's imperative that you stop and check yourself from time to time to determine if you've drifted. Think about the people you've been spending your time with and even more importantly, the people you've been listening to. Do they elevate or devastate your thinking? Remember that losers run with losers and winners run with winners. Stay on the right track! Run with the right pack!

Today I will: _____

_____

DECEMBER 21

Make your move. Chances are that you've been putting off something fairly important. It may be an attempt to rebuild a relationship with a client, learning or applying a new skill, prospecting to potential groups of customers or investing in yourself in some way. If the possibility of making a mistake is what's holding you back from trying, make your move anyway. You'll find that making any move is almost always better than paralysis. Even if you make the wrong move, you'll quickly realize it and be able to correct the course. Beginning gives you the momentum you need, so stop stalling and get on with it! Great things lie ahead!

Strategy I will use today: _____

_____

DECEMBER 22

Check your rituals. Take a hard look at them. This includes rituals for improving your skills, habits, attitudes, physical conditioning, mental conditioning, spiritual conditioning, etc. Your rituals add and reinforce balance in your life. It's important to have rituals in your personal as well as your professional life.

Needless to say, when one of these two is out of alignment it will affect everything else you try to do. Do you exercise, meditate, pray, read, listen to tapes, purposely go out and build–or rebuild–social relationships? Do you have goals with your family as well as your work? Take a hard look at whether you are so busy consuming, that you are ignoring your capacity to produce. Rituals are the key. Productive rituals don't just happen. They take thought, planning and discipline. They will also add more balance and joy to your life than anything else you can do.

Action I will take today: _____

_____

DECEMBER 23

Focus on the things you can control today. It's too easy to become a victim in sales. We get caught up and beat up by things we cannot control such as pricing, the competition, advertising, product quality, inventories, the behavior of co-workers, the decisions of management. Dwelling on or continually worrying about these matters drains your energy. It diverts your focus. It costs you sales. Focus on what you can influence, how many calls you'll make today, how many customers you will wait on, who you'll follow up with, what you'll learn, your attitude and giving presentations. Get in the habit of taking control of your day. Too many salespeople never really work at their job–they are worked by their job. They never really live their lives–they are lived by life. Turn the tables and focus on what you can control today. Let it become a habit and a way of life. Let someone else be the victim.

Today I will: _____

_____

DECEMBER 24

Take a good look at your plan for today. Are you organized? Do you have a checklist of what needs to be done? Do you have the time allotted to complete your checklist? If the answer to the previous three questions is yes, that's good. However, it still may not be enough. The problem with Time Management and to-do lists is when the things you are doing and checking off your list are not the things that give you your *greatest return*. What good does it do to blaze through your planner and list completing tasks if they are not the most important things you can do during the day? First, determine what it is you do that gives you your greatest return. This takes some honest thought. Second, schedule these things in first.

The key word here is schedule. If you are just waiting to find time to do things, they won't get done. Once you have the main things scheduled, you have a focal point from which you can either include or discard other tasks as they arise during the day. You have limited time. To get the most out of what you do, you have to put the first things first. You can work twice as long and hard on those other tasks and still not get the results you want. Work smarter on the **right** things.

Strategy I will use today: _____

_____

DECEMBER 25

Give your customers "air" today. If you were in a room listening to a speaker and the oxygen was taken from the room, would you be able to concentrate on what was being said? Of course not. Once the air was put back in the room, you'd then be ready to listen to the speaker. When we talk and talk to our customers and don't give them an adequate chance to explain their wants and needs, they feel like the person in that room without air. They won't be able to focus on what you're saying until they have it. Practice giving them air. Ask them questions–let them reply. Once they have their air, then they're ready for you.

Action I will take today: _____

_____

DECEMBER 26

Let them finish! Another listening tip is to stop finishing their sentences for them. In our haste to show that we know what they mean and understand their wants, we jump in and finish what they're saying. Not only is this rude, it's exhausting. This is because in order to do this you have to be in two heads at once–theirs and yours! Slow down, bite your tongue and give people a fair hearing; even if you know the answer. Remember, people don't buy when they understand, they buy when they feel fully understood.

Today I will: _____

_____

DECEMBER 27

Don't have all the answers too quickly. When listening to and trying to understand a customer explain their wants and needs, resist the temptation to jump in with a quick-fix answer–even if you know it's right. Listen thoughtfully and ask more questions to gain a clearer understanding of what they are saying. Besides, when you rattle off a quick, snappy answer, the customer may not have the confidence in it unless they feel you really grasp what they are saying. Would you have confidence in a doctor or attorney who gave you a "too quick" solution to your problem? Would you feel truly understood? Quick, pat answers may also unwittingly cheapen the customer's problem or situation. People like to feel special–and understood. Give them that courtesy and you'll build credibility, trust and maybe even make a friend.

Strategy I will use today: _____

_____

DECEMBER 28

Call them first. When you sense that a client has a problem or question with your product or service, take the initiative and call them first. Taking a proactive approach builds a more solid and trusting relationship. Get in the habit of soliciting your client's feedback regularly. Each call you make is another board in the bridge of the relationship with that customer. You'll be able to grow through this feedback and so will your company.

Action I will take today: _____

_____

DECEMBER 29

Fix your face. Like it or not, you set the tempo for each encounter with a customer based more on how you look than by what you say. How you say what you say is also more important than the actual words you use. How you stand and even how you walk up to greet a customer makes an immediate first impression that words alone won't be able to overcome. If you wear your emotions on your sleeve, if you carry your problems–business or personal–around on your face or in your tone or posture, you are losing sales. No one likes to deal with a deadbeat! Cheer up and shape up! Leave your problems at the curb. You are constantly on stage and on display. Make it count.

Today I will: _____

_____

December 30

"It's not what you know, it's who you know" is only part of the truth. **Who knows you** is what really counts. As a new year gets ready to begin, reflect on your personal network. Do enough people in enough places know you? Do they recommend you? What percentage of your sales is coming from repeats and referrals? If it's less than you would like, a great New Year's resolution would be to build on and aggressively expand your network. There are many good books and tapes available on how to do this. (Listed in recommended reading section in back of the book.) It will take a plan and some time, but resolve right now that the upcoming year will be the one where you double–or even triple–your repeat and referral business by expanding your customer base through networking.

Strategy I will use today: _____

_____

December 31

Add some power. A great way to add some power into your attitude and performance in the coming year would be to get rid of any inkling you have of a "scarcity mentality." This is the mindset that causes jealousy and resentment when the people you work with out-perform you. First of all, when you focus on what they are doing, you only have half your focus left to direct to what you are doing. Secondly, there is plenty to go around for everyone working hard and smart enough to get their share. Stop wasting valuable energy and attitude with grudges and bitterness. Be glad for the success of others–genuinely. Use their success as a motivator for your own goals. Let it move you closer to your highest aspirations.

Action I will take today: _____

_____

December
Month-End Action Plan

_____

_____

_____

_____

_____

_____

_____

_____

_____

_____

_____

_____

Bonus Thoughts!

Keep the faith. As you continue on your journey "Above The Crowd" during the New Year, know up front that it won't all be roses. *You will get off track!* Realizing this up front helps fight the frustration that comes with a false set of expectations. Just as an airplane is off course over 90% of the time on its way to a destination–but manages to land at the desired point, normally on time, by making course corrections–so must you. Getting off track is going to happen. It's part of the business. It's okay. Staying off track is not! Keep improving, keep correcting and you'll get to where you want to be and beyond–and you'll get there on time!

The bottom line is that the knowledge listed in the 365 strategies are of little value until you decide to turn them into action. Use the monthly Action Plans to create momentum in your daily approach to sales excellence. As you develop and improve your skills, habits and attitudes, you can probably expect a little bit of peer pressure. The "crowd" doesn't take kindly to someone who begins to rise above them. It makes them uncomfortable. Don't waste energy worrying about peer pressure you can't control. Continue to work on the areas in this book that you can control. Remember that sales excellence is a lifetime journey, not a weekend trip. Selling above the crowd is a process, not an event. Enjoy the journey!

Suggested Books & Audio Programs
For Continuing Education
And Personal Development

By Zig Ziglar:
See You At The Top
Goals
Sell Your Way To The Top
You Are A Natural Champion
Success And The Self-Image
How To Be A Winner

By Tom Hopkins:
How To Master The Art Of Selling

By Harvey Mackay:
Dig Your Well Before You're Thirsty

By Susan RoAne
The Secrets Of Savvy Networking
What Do I Say Next?

By Gerard Nierenberg
How To Read A Person Like A Book
The Art Of Negotiation

By Rick Pitino
Success Is A Choice

By Steven K. Scott
Simple Steps To Impossible Dreams

By Brian Tracy
The Psychology Of Selling
24 Techniques For Closing The Sale

The Dave Anderson Corporation

P.O. Box 2338

Agoura Hills, CA 91376

Phone: 800-519-8224 or 818-735-9979 *(Outside of U.S.)*

Fax: 818-735-0299

E-mail: Dave@LearnToLead.com

Website: www.LearnToLead.com

Important: Copyright Warning!

About The Author

Dave Anderson is president of The Dave Anderson Corporation and *LearnToLead.com*. His companies provide sales, management and leadership training, publications and consulting to businesses internationally.

Dave started his career in sales as a teen-ager selling car care products at the annual auto expositions in New York and Chicago. He has been a car salesman, general manager and director of some of the most successful automotive dealerships in the U.S. Dave is the author of over 50 sales and leadership training programs, including the books, *Selling Above The Crowd: 365 Strategies For Sales Excellence, No-Nonsense Leadership, Up Your Business,* and *If You Don't Make Waves You'll Drown: 10 Hard-Charging Strategies for Leading in Politically Correct Times.* He publishes a monthly newsletter, *Leading At The Next Level* and authors a monthly leadership column for *DEALER* magazine. His website, www.learntolead.com provides free training articles and information to thousands of clients each week in over 30 countries and his business writings are regularly featured on top sales and leadership web sites each month.

Dave conducts 150 speeches, workshops and presentations internationally each year. He continues to be a favorite, featured speaker at the annual N.A.D.A. convention and is a member of the National Speakers Association. His numerous cassette programs, email services, book and other publications are available at his website, www.learntolead.com or at Amazon.com.

Dave's training pulls no punches and gets results in today's marketplace. Dave is a leader who has personally led many organizations to new levels and consults with many of the top sales organizations in the world. His real world perspective comes through in strategies that are immediately applicable and geared toward lasting results.

Dave Anderson resides in Agoura Hills, California.

Join The Insider Club!

Get free sales, management and leadership articles and advice at www.LearnToLead.com! New information is added often to help you reach your full potential